BASIC HISTORY
OF AMERICAN BUSINESS

THOMAS C. COCHRAN

Professor of History
University of Pennsylvania

AN ANVIL ORIGINAL

under the general editorship of

LOUIS L. SNYDER

D. VAN NOSTRAND COMPANY, INC.

PRINCETON, NEW JERSEY

TORONTO   LONDON

NEW YORK

D. VAN NOSTRAND COMPANY, INC.
120 Alexander St., Princeton, New Jersey (*Principal office*); 24 West 40 St., New York, N.Y.
D. VAN NOSTRAND COMPANY (Canada), LTD.
25 Hollinger Rd., Toronto 16, Canada
D. VAN NOSTRAND COMPANY, LTD.
358, Kensington High Street, London, W.14, England

Library of Congress Catalog Card No. 59-9759

PREFACE

How should a basic history of American business differ from the numerous economic histories of the United States? To begin with, economic history is to a large extent a series of measurements of material progress expressed in dollars of imports, thousands of cotton spindles, or miles of track, whereas business history is primarily a record of ideas, customs, and organizations. The stage on which the businessman plays his role is set by current technology and economic possibilities, but these are only the scenery; the "business" of the play is business. Since it deals with the reactions of individuals to personal challenges and opportunities, business history is a humanistic as well as a social science study. The moves of Commodore Vanderbilt cannot be charted adequately by social psychology or economic norms; they have also to be seen as responses to American culture and, in the end, simply described as the behavior of a unique human being.

In this brief survey the conventional economic background must be held to the barest minimum and attention focused only on the new adventures of business leaders in organizing and managing economic life. It will be necessary to make many overly simple generalizations, which could be properly modified in a longer book, to speak often of businessmen as one group, which they seldom are, and to concentrate on a few fundamentals to the neglect of the vast intricacy of business processes.

Philadelphia, Pa. THOMAS C. COCHRAN
February, 1959

TABLE OF CONTENTS

Part 1

BASIC HISTORY OF AMERICAN BUSINESS

— 1 —

THE BUSINESS OF COLONIZATION

The Merchant Adventurers. In the last years of the reign of Queen Elizabeth I, England entered her long era of imperial greatness. All parts of English life seemed charged with a new energy. Shakespeare was writing his plays, Bacon his philosophy and science, Drake and Frobisher were carrying out their fabulous naval actions, and the businessmen of the English ports were aspiring to draw off the wealth of the world. Men enriched by trade were mingling with the aristocracy and the professions to create a business group which combined vision, influence, and enterprise.

The times encouraged overoptimism. Spain had netted millions in gold and silver from her colonies. Early English trade ventures were bringing profits undreamed of fifty years before. In 1600 Thomas Smith and his associates won a charter from the Queen for an East India Company. Setting up each trip to the East as a separate venture, the stockholders divided profits that averaged over 100 per cent a voyage.

It was hoped that North America would prove as rich in gold and silver as Mexico or Peru, as good a source of silks and spices as China or India. Seagull, a character in Marston's play, *Westward Ho,* showing in London in 1605, said of Virginia: "I tell thee, golde is more plentiful there than copper is with us. . . . Why man, all their dripping pans and chamber pots are pure gold; and all the chains with which they chain up their streets are made of gold . . . and for rubies and diamonds they goe forth on holy days and gather them by the seashore." Business leaders took a more sober view, but they too thought in terms of large profits from small investments. Thus the origins of American business were in the ventures of wealthy Englishmen. The early settlements were enterprises conceived not by the government for imperial purposes, but by entrepreneurs for private profit.

The Calvinist Influence. The Puritans or, more broadly, people of Calvinist religious leanings, including Presbyterians, Quakers, and other minor sects were a powerful influence in both English business and American colonization. While Puritans would "purify" and simplify the ritual of the Church of England, they reluctantly took part in "low" Episcopal services. The other dissenters more closely followed the doctrines of divinely predetermined salvation or damnation preached by John Calvin of Geneva, Switzerland. They were allowed to worship at their own churches but still had to pay taxes for the support of the Anglican ministry.

Since dissent was strong in the larger cities, many of the merchants interested in colonization were Calvinists. Their doctrines were particularly suited to early business. They emphasized economy and simplicity in both church and society. Man was expected to busy himself on earth, and what the righteous did was God's work. One must carefully choose a calling in which the talents bestowed by God would be best utilized. Worldly success was a sign of God's grace, an assurance of everlasting life. The money made should not be wasted on extravagant ostentatious living. After allotting the church its share, the remainder should be used in furthering one's useful ventures which were also God's.

These doctrines were shaped by the desires of the businessmen of the rising commercial centers. Religion thus became a weapon to be used against the waste and extravagance of kings and nobles who dissipated the sinews of economic growth. It was no accident that the resulting doctrines were almost perfectly attuned to the needs of a young expanding capitalism. Personal gain, social good, and God's will became one and the same.

Colonial Companies. In 1606, King James I gave a charter to two groups of promoters from Plymouth and London to colonize, respectively, the northern and southern parts of the Atlantic coast. The next year the Londoners landed a boatload of colonists on the coast of Virginia and named the settlement Jamestown.

The blending of motives that inspired these English businessmen to risk their capital in this venture is illustrated in the concluding paragraph of instructions to the first colonizing expedition: "Lastly and chiefly, the way to prosper and achieve good success is to make yourselves all of one mind for the good of your country and your own, and to serve and fear God the Giver of all Goodness, for every plantation which our Heavenly Father hath not planted shall be rooted out." [1]

During the seventeenth century, settlement was attempted by chartered companies, unincorporated associations, partnerships, and proprietors, but all met similar economic and managerial difficulties, and all were unsuccessful as business ventures. In theory, profits were to come from sending settlers who would catch fish, trade with the Indians for furs, and possibly develop other local products. In some colonies the settlers were small stockholders in the English company, in others they were employees or servants; but in all cases the investors in England expected to own most of the property and to receive most of the profits. Lured by such hopes, English capitalists sank fortunes in colonies that progressed too slowly and poorly for profitable returns. As in later cases of premature or inadequate investment in railroads, canals, mines, and town sites, society ultimately reaped benefits from the financial sacrifices of the pioneers.

There were no quick sources of wealth on the Atlantic seaboard—no jewels, no mines of precious metals, no rich natives to be plundered. There were only moderately fertile farm lands to be cleared of trees and broken to the plow, only small supplies of fur near the coast and these to be bought from crafty Indians who controlled the back country, and only fish that had to be caught by dangerous voyages in the cold and stormy waters of the northern coast. Of these three, fish and fur promised the quickest returns, but land was the easiest to control as a monopoly by absentee managers, and hence should be a source of steady income.

That turkeys, boars, deer, and smaller animals filled

[1] Edward D. Neill, *History of the Virginia Company of London* (Joel Munsell, Albany, 1869), pp. 13-14.

the forest, that great flocks of game birds darkened the skies, and that virgin soil promised good crops were of little value for dividends. Aside from fish, England and the rest of Europe grew their own food. Only some exotic crop, such as silk, indigo, or tobacco, would have immediate export value. Furthermore, the fertility of virgin soil was offset by lack of adequate farm equipment, by new diseases for which settlers lacked immunity, by colder winters than they had known at home, and by Indian attacks resulting from ill-considered policies. All of these disadvantages would lessen eventually, but not fast enough to satisfy absentee stockholders.

Different plans for turning royal land grants into ready cash for colonial development were tried by various promoters. The Virginia Company, a chartered corporation, tried to raise cash by selling stock at £12.10s., par value, reckoned as the cost of transporting a settler, with a land grant as a bonus. Men who could pay for their own equipment and transportation would become stockholders in the company with land grants proportional to the number of people they brought with them. (*See Reading No. 1.*) Dividends on the stock were to come from control of the trade of the colony. By 1612, when the colony needed further investment and stock would no longer sell in the English market, lotteries became "the real and substantial food" for nourishing the Jamestown settlement.

Although the company never made a profit, the ultimate surrender of its rights to the crown, representing a loss to the stockholders of some £100,000, was also the result of a long political quarrel among the directors in London. A Puritan faction, led by Sir Edwin Sandys, battled the orthodox group led by Sir Thomas Smith until the dissolution of the company in 1624.

Similar arrangements were entered into by unchartered associations. Seventy English "Adventurers" financed the voyage of the Pilgrims to Plymouth. These unfortunate London merchants put up £7,000 in £10 shares in return for the proceeds of the labor of 102 colonists over the next seven years. Then a division was to be made of all the property with the settlers sharing as members of the company. (*See Reading No. 1.*)

The company agents pursued fishing and Indian trade

in beaver, but mismanagement and misfortune brought ruin. The French captured the first return cargo, and the Turks a valuable one a few years later. The settlement was inadequately supplied with trade goods and was far from the sources of fur, but the company would not permit a move. At the end of seven years the London promoters were willing to sell out to the colonists for the accumulated debt of the venture, £1,800. From this and similar enterprises it was becoming obvious that fish and fur could not supply the funds needed for the building of a colony profitable to British investors.

To move and establish each farmer cost at least £10 or $50.00. Since no English working man had any such sum, the capital had to be advanced by the promoters. (*See Reading No. 1.*) This meant $5,000 for each hundred households, and this was only the beginning. For three or four years the farmers, having to build houses and barns, clear the forest, break the soil with wooden plows, provide public buildings and protect themselves against the Indians, were likely to need substantial help. Fur trading posts had to be constructed at distant strategic points in order to reach Indians ahead of competitors from other settlements. Wharves and ships for fishing were an additional drain, and one that might occur again and again as storms wrecked the port.

Some New England settlements, such as Massachusetts Bay and New Haven, prospered because substantial property owners came for religious reasons and invested their personal capital in developing the colony. The total of these sums, let alone their better management, probably exceeded the amount that could have been raised by the sale of company securities. The Massachusetts Bay Company was the outstanding example of a migration by substantial property owners. Led by John Winthrop, a Puritan gentleman, the stockholders voted in 1629 to move the company to Massachusetts. Those stockholders who did not want to migrate were compensated by land grants and certain concessions over the next seven years, but there were to be no dividends on any shares. A goodly company of prosperous Puritans sold their holdings in England and accompanied Winthrop on the voyage to Boston.

The Proprietors.   In spite of the lack of profit from early settlements, English investors could not be convinced that there was no money in developing the fertile lands that the King was willing to give to promoters of settlement. Consequently, men of wealth like Lord Baltimore, Captain John Mason, and Sir Edmund Plowden continued to petition the crown for grants of land in America. There was one striking difference, however, between these grants to proprietors and the earlier ones to merchant adventurers. The merchants had expected profit from trade and special products, the proprietors looked to an income from land sales and quit rents.

The term "quit rent," meaning a fixed annual tax, brings out a new nonbusiness aspect of these proprietary grants. The land came as a feudal fief from the crown, and the grantee became a direct tenant or vassal of the King. In return for a token annual payment to the King, such as two arrowheads or some beaver skins, the proprietor had the right to govern, tax, and sell the land that had been granted. Thus, regardless of profit, he became the ruler of a vast domain; he could thrill to the power of feudal lordship in the medieval sense. This helps to explain why English gentlemen ruined themselves in seeking to establish colonies.

As we have seen, this was no game for men of small means. From 1632 on, Cecilius Calvert, Baron Baltimore, invested more than £30,000 in the development of Maryland before receiving any net return. William Penn claimed to have invested a like sum in Pennsylvania from 1680 to 1698 without profit, and ultimately he had to assign the Pennsylvania revenues to his creditors in order to secure his release from debtors prison. Twenty years earlier eight proprietors sunk some £20,000 in the Carolinas. Of all of these feudal lords of the Atlantic coast only the Calverts and the Penns retained their powers of government down to the Revolution. In the later years they drew an income from quit rents, but the later returns never equaled the value of the principal and interest that might have accrued from some safer but less romantic investment.

English entrepreneurs were not the only ones to lose

money along the North Atlantic coast. The Dutch and the Swedes, neither known for reckless speculation, failed to establish profitable colonies. The trading post of the Swedish South Company on the Delaware fell to the Dutch in the course of a European war in 1655. Dutch settlements, in turn, including New Amsterdam, were conquered by the English in 1664. But in neither case was the colony worth defending from a business standpoint.

In all the finance of colonial settlement, even that of Massachusetts and Pennsylvania, there ran a strong element of business interest. The backers of the Pilgrims expected to make money. John Winthrop and his wealthy fellow migrants to Massachusetts Bay hoped also to better themselves financially. William Penn wished not only to provide a haven for Quakers, but to build a great estate for his heirs. British America was settled during an upsurge of European business, on what was hoped to be a businesslike basis. This meant that, from the beginning, business considerations, as distinct from feudal or religious, had a secure and honorable place in American life, and businessmen enjoyed far more prestige than in the aristocratic monarchies of the Old World.

— 2 —

THE LIFE OF TRADE

The Merchant. Looking out over Boston's central market square from his shop at Cornhill and King streets, Robert Keayne must have felt satisfaction with his success. Like the other colonial merchants of the 1630's he was a self-made man. His father had been a butcher and he, having "no portion from my parents or friends to begin the world withal," worked his way up through apprenticeship to be a merchant tailor in London. But in England, despite his modest fortune of two or three thousand pounds, he was still nobody, a petty tradesman beneath the notice of the gentry. Coming to Boston in 1635 and engaging in overseas trade, he soon became an important figure in the community. His brother-in-law was a member of the powerful Puritan clergy; he was a freeman of the corporation and played a leading part in local affairs.

Good English connections, which meant friends in a substantial export house that would extend long-term credit, was the usual basis for mercantile success in the colonies. The flood of immigrants in the decade of the thirties, 20,000 to New England alone, created a continuous, almost desperate demand for goods. But most of those who wished to buy had nothing to offer but promises to be redeemed in fish, fur, butter, or meat. The merchant who could carry such accounts by advances from England could charge high prices and reap great profits from struggling farmers and fishermen. The hand of the merchant was seen everywhere. He lent money, ran distilleries, and slaughterhouses, owned ships, and controlled the town councils. (*See Reading No. 2.*)

It was not surprising that such men aroused public jealousy and resentment. This was to be the historic lot of big businessmen in democratic America. But the first generation of New Englanders had special reasons for disliking and distrusting merchants. The independent traders who fitted out vessels to buy and sell to the early settlements, often in defiance of company regulations, were mainly unscrupulous manipulators with no respectable place in the world of English business. Taking advantage of shortages, they sold inferior goods at outrageous prices, they secured furs cheap by selling arms and liquor to the Indians, in short, in a strict and highly religious country, these merchants appeared to have neither manners nor ethics. In the early 1630's, three unscrupulous London merchants received £10,000 worth of furs from the Pilgrims in Plymouth and were later discovered to have made off with all but £600 of the proceeds.

The Massachusetts Bay settlers attracted the first merchants with good English connections and interest in building the business of the colony. But while men such as Keayne were honest, they were not averse to taking full advantage of the ups and downs of the market in both prices and interest rates. In contrast, the Puritan theocracy advocated "just" price and regard for one's neighbor. Asked what rule should be obeyed in lending, Governor Winthrop said: "Thou must observe whether thy brother hath present or possible means of repaying thee, if ther be none of these, thou must give him according to his necessity . . ."

As European war and rapid immigration led to inflation in the late 1630's, the Bay Colony attempted to fix prices. Keayne and other merchants refused to be bound by these rulings of God's chosen representatives when they conflicted with the laws of the market. As a result, he was singled out for exemplary punishment. Publicly condemned by the General Court, and fined £200, he thought the feeling against him was so bitter that "if some could have had their wills they would have the fyne mounted up to 1000 lb." (*See Reading No. 11.*)

Regardless of regulations both British and Colonial, or public ill-will, the merchants of all sections grew steadily in wealth and prestige. In a country where many necessities and most luxuries had to be imported, the man of overseas trade performed the most important business function. After the restoration of the Stuart kings in 1660, the New England merchants gained power while the authority of the church declined. In New York and Philadelphia, the merchants were leaders from the start. In Baltimore, Williamsburg, Norfolk, and Charleston, merchants mingled socially with the planters, who often were in trade themselves.

The term "merchant" was generally reserved for men conducting wholesale overseas trade, as distinct from mere shopkeepers. The unpretentious office of a leading merchant, looking like a general store with some extra desks and account books squeezed in, was a center of colonial business. Goods of all kinds were stored in the merchants' warehouse and small quantities put on sale in the shop. Few merchants were strictly wholesalers.

Retail customers as well as shopkeepers came to purchase supplies.

Throughout the colonial period, money was scarce or unobtainable for everyday transactions. Even an important eighteenth-century merchant like Thomas Hancock would not be surprised to see a farmer drive up to the shop next to Faneuil Hall in Boston with a wagon load of corn, poultry, and flour, a calf on a rope and two or three pigs with which to pay for his fall supplies. Since the merchant had so often to barter his goods, he sought to pay his bills the same way. A carpenter was paid for repair work on Hancock's house with "a gun, cider, barrels of beef, pencils, candles, hogs, molasses and wood."

The twine that kept this business world from falling apart completely was book credit. Pigs and cows did not have to match guns and cloth in every transaction. Each had a price on the books of the merchant, and buyers and sellers ran debits and credits that were never completely balanced from one year to the next. To be in debt to someone was to insure their patronage, because only by buying goods could the debt be discharged. This "bookkeeping barter" was the salvation of trade and explains the occasional "carrying of coal to Newcastle" or, more specifically, shipping fish to New England or butter to Ireland, when these were all the merchant could find for the discharge of his obligation.

Since northern merchants wanted to buy much more from England than they could pay for in the produce of their own colonies, elaborate roundabout trades resulted. If, for example, Thomas Hancock and his wife did not want to eat the farmer's calf or hogs, they might send them to the Spanish West Indies where meat could be sold, and receive, in addition to molasses, or sugar, some Spanish milled dollars. These were the principal coins to reach the colonies. British guineas, crowns, or shillings appeared on account books, but were scarcely ever in anyone's pocket. Good bills on English merchants had too high an exchange rate to be attractive means of payment. Only the extension of bookkeeping barter by British correspondents made trade possible. The colonial merchant usually had large balances due in England which he struggled to liquidate in whale oil or bones, sugar or molasses, tobacco or rice, or products from other parts of the world.

To ease the money problem at home, the separate colonies became pioneers in the issue of paper money. Usually it came into circulation as mortgage money loaned by a government agency. Redemption was to come from taxes within a set period. But taxes in specie were as hard to collect as mercantile debts. The redemption periods were postponed, and more money was issued. By 1750 the notes of the various colonies were passing at a confusing variety of rates of depreciation. Pennsylvania pounds, for example, were near par, while those of Massachusetts were worth less than 10 per cent of their face value in English money. The paper, useless abroad, provided a domestic medium of exchange, but greatly complicated the interpretation of colonial accounts.

The operations of real estate, banking, investment, and insurance went through the merchant's office. Because of his connections with correspondents abroad he was in a position to buy or sell bills on foreign cities, arrange for mortgage money, order foreign securities for investors, and participate in marine insurance underwriting.

Except for an increasing scale of operations and a tendency toward specialization in certain trade or business, the operations of the merchant scarcely changed over a two-hundred year period. Prior to 1790 roads were of little use for shipping bulky goods and, since few colonists lived more than 25 miles from navigable water, even domestic trade was by ship. Merchants usually owned their ships, although to spread risk each vessel might be jointly held by several partners who were not otherwise associated. Sometimes individual voyages were set up as partnership ventures to be liquidated from the proceeds of the return cargo. There were some long-term partnerships such as that of Willing and Morris in Philadelphia, but more often a merchant ran his own business with the help of one or two relatives.

The ships of the merchant ranged from the Mediterranean to the North Sea, from Africa to the Caribbean, as well as from Florida to Nova Scotia. (*See Reading No. 2.*) While the exchange of colonial raw materials for British manufacturers was the most important single trade, that with the West Indies was always large. A New England merchant could send salt fish and home manufactures to Charleston, instructing his captain to pick up barrel staves, rice and meat for the West Indies. There the captain would exchange the Charleston goods for molasses, sugar, ginger, and fruit and return home. A longer variant of the southern trip was to carry rum from New England to Africa, bring slaves back to the West Indies, and sugar and molasses back home.

Merchants in the northern colonies lacking the tobacco, rice, and indigo that served their southern neighbors for export to England, might send fish to one of the Catholic countries of Europe, carry some varied cargo from there to England, and then stock British articles for the voyage home. New Englanders with fish and whale oil for export leaned toward continental European trade, merchants of the middle colonies did best in the export of food and lumber to the West Indies, while the southerners could profitably export their tobacco and rice direct to England.

All these trades were somewhat restricted by British laws, but since the laws were not enforced they were generally disregarded. One was not supposed, for example, to import Spanish or French West Indian molasses without paying a prohibitive duty, but this never stopped a shrewd captain from buying where molasses was cheapest and falsifying the invoice.

The loyalty and ability of captains, supercargoes, and correspondents in foreign ports were obviously keys to the success of complicated trading voyages. On small vessels, the captain performed the business in addition to being master of the ship. For larger ventures, a business agent, or supercargo, represented the merchant. Loyalty to the owner was the most necessary quality in a supercargo. Operating thousands of miles and months of time away from the home office there was no way of keeping a check on his activities. He might trade on his own account to the detriment of his master or falsify sales. For this reason, relatives whose interests were identified with the business were often preferred to more talented outsiders.

Merchants neither faced the problem of coordinating workers and administrators, nor were forced to develop systematic ideas regarding management. The captains hired and fired the crews that operated the ships, and the merchant needed few men for his office and warehouse. Two or three porters to move goods to and from the warehouse, and one or two clerks to tend the goods on display and to keep the books were sufficient.

Bookkeeping had scarcely changed since the Renaissance. If no divisions had to be made between partners, no balances were struck. No income taxes forced calculations of profit and loss. Daily transactions were entered in a journal, often in different types of money with household and office expenses mixed together. In transferring accounts to a ledger probably only the largest and most meticulous merchants used a double entry system.

The pace of business life was geared to the leisurely coming and going of sailing ships with few transactions each day. Aside from much letter writing to foreign correspondents there was little pressure on office work. The merchant, after a late midday dinner, could often spend his afternoons in taverns or coffee houses discussing common business concerns with his competitors, ride around inspecting his property, or sit at home over a game of cards or chess.

Insurance and Investment. In the seventeenth and early eighteenth centuries, the coffee houses, a more polite word than tavern, substituted for stock exchanges, insurance agencies, chambers of commerce, and brokerage offices. Different establishments became associated with different types of activity. Those wishing to buy or sell government bonds or the securities of joint stock companies would gather at a certain coffee house, others wishing to place insurance on vessels bound for Europe might regularly go to another, while real estate trading went on at all gatherings.

By the end of the eighteenth century, both marine and fire insurance offices had been organized in London and some Americans arranged marine coverage by mail, but underwriting in the colonies was still on the basis of individual arrangements. Successful organization of this service may have required newspapers. At any rate, in 1721, two years after the beginning of the publication of *The American Weekly Mercury,* the second Colonial newspaper, an advertisement appeared for a marine insurance office. At his house on High Street, in the business center of Philadelphia, John Copson was prepared to arrange for insurance on "Vessels, Goods and Merchandizes." He undertook to find insurers of "Undoubted Worth and Reputation." These early insurance agencies probably followed the same system that had been used informally among merchants. The shipper made out a policy stipulating the voyage, the amount, and the rate he would pay, and then capitalists ready to risk their money stopped by and underwrote varying fractions of the whole.

While marine insurance continued to be arranged through brokers, in 1752 Benjamin Franklin, a veteran volunteer fireman, led the way to establishing a mutual fire insurance company known as the Philadelphia Contributorship for the Insurance of Houses from Loss by Fire. Although earlier attempts at fire insurance in Boston and Charleston had failed, Franklin's venture succeeded. It was not followed by companies in other colonies, however, and insurance continued to be arranged through brokers or in coffee houses.

The one type of investment that appealed to all capitalists was land. To be a successful merchant required a keen mind for values and prospects, and involved continual risks on sea and land. To attempt manufacturing necessitated special skill and careful supervision, and even then profits were uncertain. To run a retail shop or tavern consumed all one's time. But, to own and rent land required little exertion, and if selected with only reasonable sagacity urban and ex-urban property continually increased in value. City houses, rented for commercial purposes, brought a reliable income that could keep pace with the long-run trend of inflation. Consequently, successful merchants limited their commitments in trade and put their surplus profits into real estate. This not only insured a growing inheritance for their children, but increased their own standing in the community. The history of Philadelphia, particularly, where the surrounding farming land was rich, is one of Quaker merchant families evolving into Episcopalian landed gentry.

The Craftsmen. Nearly all manufacturing in the colonies was done in the craftsman's house. Nine men out of ten were farmers who made everything possible at home. Soap, candles, clothing, and liquor were seldom bought. A spinning wheel for wool and flax and a hand loom were conventional articles of living-room furniture. Only occasionally would a trip to the general store in the nearest village be necessary. Then hogs or poultry or cider might be traded for farm or household implements, cloth, or whale oil. If the farmer was far from a village he might rely most of the time on chapmen or peddlers who came with immense saddlebags full of hardware, cloth, and knickknacks. Traveling cordwainers would make the farmer's calfskin into shoes, traveling chandlers with molds would make the farmer's tallow into candles, and traveling limners would paint his picture.

Flour and saw milling with water wheels run by small streams, and blacksmithing were universal country businesses, often combined with farming on the side. A miller, called in from his field, would start the wheels to grind a few bushels of wheat, and then resume his farm work. A local blacksmith would fashion hinges, tools, and kitchen utensils as well as shoe horses and mend wagons.

How to pay these businessmen was an endless problem. Farmers living near populous towns, which were very few even in the mid-eighteenth century, might sell their garden truck or grain products to merchants. Those living farther away could drive animals to market on the hoof. But most New England and back-country farmers had little surplus. Thus craftsmen had to accept the varied products of self-sufficient farms, such as brandy, wine, cloth or food.

Even southern planters with access to navigable water and staple crops for export tried to be as nearly self-sufficient as practicable. To free the planter from the clutches of grasping merchants and the costs of importation, slaves were taught to do scores of specialized handicrafts.

In and around the coastal ports, however, craftsmen aided by apprentices, journeymen, wives, and children pursued their specialties. The lower floor of the house was the workshop and salesroom combined. By the early eighteenth century there were few of the manifold wants of a prosperous urban society that could not be supplied locally. American craftsmen were recruited from Germany, Holland, France, and Switzerland as well as from the British Isles. Bringing mature skills from the manufacturing centers of the Old World, their foreign training was advertised as a business asset. The colonial cities had London tailors, French peruke-makers, German metal workers, and scores of other transplanted artisans.

As in other societies of a prefactory age, apparel and furniture were the chief types of manufacture. The craftsmen of different cities who developed special skills and designs began to command a market in nearby colonies as well as in the West Indies. Philadelphia leather breeches, or Windsor chairs, or Boston Silverware sold up and down the coast and in the islands.

Lack of power machinery was only one of several factors that limited most manufacturing to a single household. Men had to acquire the necessary hand skills by apprenticeship and it was unusual for them to have access to much capital. A master craftsman setting up a new shop, as did many immigrants, could rent a house, but needed from £5 to £100 worth of equipment. The average may have been around £50 sterling, the equivalent of more than $1,000 in the 1950's. For a workingman this was a large sum, and tended to make such proprietorships hereditary, sons taking over the equipment of their fathers. In addition, the old guild system—payment to the city for a "freedom" to operate—was continued in some colonies. But such taxes were steadily lightened and loosely enforced.

As in all American operations, labor was extremely scarce. The English rule of a seven-year apprenticeship had to be relaxed to four or even three years. Lodged by the master in his own household, the apprentices were under a monastic discipline. Few recreations were permitted without the consent of the master. It is likely that, except for men and boys who apprenticed themselves to pay for their passage to the colonies, or convicts who were working off a prison sentence, most apprentices were relatives or the sons of friends. For training and discipline, masters in the same craft would apprentice their sons to each other. But all sources together supplied too few beginners, and thus held down the size of operations. Masters continually advertised for apprentices and offered bonuses in clothing and supplies at the completion of the term.

Good journeymen were harder to find and keep than good apprentices. Probably the average household establishment had no journeymen, their place being taken by wives and other members of the family. The fact that journeymen's wages generally included board and lodging deprived them of independence. As a result, men who remained in this status were likely to be those handicapped by drunkenness or lacking in vigor and initiative. There was little to hold the journeyman to any one job. If he wished to be rid of his wife or seek new adventures, he could always move to the next city and readily find employment.

This system made it easy and natural for widows to continue their husband's business. There was no type of small-scale enterprise without its female entrepreneurs. Not only were they tavern and shopkeepers, but tanners, metal workers, and smiths. That these female activities were taken as a matter of course shows the essential family character of business enterprise.

Another limitation on size was smallness of the market. In general, competition limited sales to the area within walking distance of the shop. There customers expected to find the craftsman at work six days a week from dawn to dusk, ready to take orders or sell at retail. Advertising in the local papers might in some cases spread the market to the metropolitan area, but only extra skillful entrepreneurs succeeded in developing export trade to other cities.

The responsibility for success or failure in his struggle against nearby competitors rested squarely on the master. He had to train and educate his apprentices and journeymen whose skill largely determined the rate of profit. With the help of his wife he ran a boarding house for the workers. He kept books, designed the products, and handled sales promotion. It must have been a rare entrepreneur who could perform all of these tasks efficiently.

The limited size of most competitive markets, and the large amount of activity by governments regulating the quality, measures, and prices of essential commodities and services held back the formation of trade associations until late in the colonial period. The Philadelphia organization of master carpenters in 1724 and that of the Boston barbers in the same year are the only exceptions. With only fifteen or twenty craftsmen competing in the same area, prices may have been adjusted in informal talks.

Larger Enterprises. Because of the possibilities of gaining a wide market by distinctive design or quality or because of the size of the equipment needed, some crafts lent themselves to a larger scale of operation. Tailors, printers, or silversmiths, for example, won intercolonial markets by superior design or quality; shipbuilders or iron manufacturers required an increasing amount of expensive equipment.

Benjamin Franklin, a craftsman of rare ability, based a large fortune on success in the printing trade. Like most colonial printers he was also a publisher. The *Pennsylvania Gazette* and *Poor Richards Almanac,* published annually from 1732 to 1764, made more money than job printing. Exploiting other angles of his business, he sponsored mills to which he sold rags and from which he received finished paper. He marketed this in turn to printing establishments up and down the coast, in many of which he had a partnership interest. While his intellectual brilliance made him a leading figure, first of Philadelphia and then of the western world, for many years he emphasized his craftsman's diligence and simplicity. When he received new type from London, he went to the dock with a wheelbarrow and pushed it back to the shop. (*See Reading No. 2.*)

Shipyards, centered around the northern ports, grew larger as time went on. Building a ship was an assembly business, rope, hardware, lumber, and other fittings being purchased from their manufacturers. But increasingly big yard owners took over more and more of these manufactures themselves. In many ways, coordinating the work of a large shipyard was the nearest approach in the eighteenth century to the problems of later factory management.

There were some iron works in the major cities, but generally iron manufacture was a country business determined by the juxtaposition of ore, limestone, and timber. The investment necessary for a furnace, bloomerie, and forge for producing bar iron was far beyond the means of an ordinary craftsman. Three thousand pounds sterling would finance only a small operation. Consequently, partnerships were formed by large landowners and merchants. From the early eighteenth century on, works appeared wherever the necessary supplies were discovered. By 1750, in defiance of British regulations against plating and slitting mills in the colonies, a large and well-equipped iron industry had been built by American entrepreneurs, many of whom made large fortunes. (*See Reading No. 11.*)

Every able colonial businessman sought new types of enterprise that might yield a profit. Silversmiths sold liquor as well as cups. Tavern keepers developed sidelines such as watch repairing. In addition to exploiting iron deposits, large landowners like William Trent built grist or saw mills, which in his case formed the nucleus of Trenton, New Jersey.

A Business-like Society. Thus, aside from a few crafts with demanding skills, the Colonial period was an age in which businessmen had many interests. Although the activities of merchants were generally the most varied and important, covering transportation, banking, finance, insurance, and marketing, this wide range did not clearly distinguish them from many other entrepreneurs. In a mobile society on the edge of a continent inviting development, men seized upon the opportunities around them. Rank and occupation were no barriers to expansion into new lines. The great tobacco planter might become interested in iron, or the merchant in flour milling and shipbuilding, while the shipbuilder might add a smithy or a rope walk. The fine gentleman from a country estate, riding in his coach dressed in velvet and lace, might be a partner in a general store down at the wharves. No social stigma was attached to participating as an owner or master in any legal occupation.

— 3 —

A NATIONAL BUSINESS SYSTEM

Tacking around Cape May with a northeastern blowing from a lowering sky the sailor might think of New York as a distant port. There could be a week of buffeting off the Jersey coast before a sloop reached the Narrows. Even by land, Philadelphia and New York, separated by ninety-five miles and two large rivers, were far apart. In the mid-eighteenth century it took three sixteen-hour days of bumping in an iron-tired stagecoach to make the trip. No bulky goods went by land.

In spite of intercolonial trade in some items, each major port with its tributary back country was a separate business community remote from its neighbors. The personal ties that bound the business world together were more often between American merchants and the houses of Liverpool and London than between men on this side of the Atlantic. Businessmen of Charleston were more at home in London than in Boston. No common stocks, bonds, or currencies, no trading corporations, banks, or insurance companies united these nearby cities separated by treacherous roads and dangerous seas.

Imperial Regulations. The force that was to create an Atlantic coast business world within a single generation was opposition to Great Britain. Goaded by British taxes, merchants and lawyers from many cities met together in Boston, New York, or Philadelphia, planned strategies of defense, signed nonimportation agreements, or devised substitutes for British trade and credit.

The trouble started in 1763 at the end of the Seven Years' War. In London a young Tory minister tried to

make the imperial administration self-supporting, a task
made doubly difficult by a British civil service staffed
by inactive gentlemen and their corrupt assistants. To
produce more revenue, tariff duties were to be collected,
by the navy if necessary. To confine trade to taxable
channels, imports prohibited by law, such as Madeira
wine brought direct from Spain or her possessions, were
to be prevented in fact. Legal documents were to be
written on stamped papers of various values. The resulting cash, which it was hoped would accrue to the government, rather than remain in the pockets of venal revenue
officers, would pay for the military, naval, and other services deemed necessary to govern and protect the North
American colonies.

But the colonists wanted no part of the new system.
The French had lost control of Canada and the Spaniards
had lost Florida; the only need for defense was against the
Indians, and British forces were seldom useful for this
purpose. Only by defying the law, argued many substantial merchants, had Americans been able to make a
living by trade. To tax or prohibit trade with the French
and Spanish areas would be to stop the inward flow of
money with which British goods were bought. To collect
duties offshore by naval searches would be to deny to
the colonists the rights of Englishmen.

More ominous still to lawyers, real estate operators,
and men of property was the precedent of an internal
stamp tax. Once established, internal taxes could be end-
lessly increased at the whim of a British Parliament in
which the colonists had no representation. Not only were
the colonies not represented, argued smart lawyers like
John Adams, but rightly they were not even under the
jurisdiction of Parliament. Each colony belonged to the
King as part of his personal heritage, and he should
rule in each through its assembly just as he ruled in
Great Britain through Parliament.

The full elaboration of such delicate constitutional
arguments took a few years, but, meanwhile, the mercantile situation seemed desperate. In the winter of 1764
and 1765 the colonies had sunk into a postwar depression.
The tight credit situation was aggravated by another Act
of Parliament prohibiting the further emission of paper

money by the colonial governments. Lawyers and local politicians, seizing the opportunity to become leaders for colonial rights, had relatively little difficulty in getting city merchants, who were short of cash anyway, to sign agreements not to import from Great Britain.

Meanwhile, public sentiment against the stamp tax rose spontaneously and was whipped up higher by colonial Whig leaders and their mass organization called the "Sons of Liberty." Tax offices were smashed and stamped paper destroyed. Transactions were recorded on ordinary foolscap in defiance of the law. Clearly something must be done to preserve property and order. At this juncture the more conservative Whig businessmen, planters, and lawyers called an intercolonial Congress to meet in New York and present their cause to the British government. As a result of this, plus the more potent pressure of English mercantile houses, the stamp tax was repealed in 1765. (*See Reading No. 3.*) Although tariff duties remained as a source of conflict, nonimportation was temporarily abandoned.

New British revenue duties in 1767 brought new nonimportation agreements. Although many merchants refused to sign such agreements and many who signed did not observe them, this political activity was bringing businessmen together. Leading defenders of colonial rights like the Adamses and John Hancock of Boston came for the first time to know who was who among the merchants and lawyers of New York and Philadelphia. To knit together the more militant spirits in each port, Committees of Correspondence were established. Thus, in the years between 1763 and 1774, fostered by depression and British pressures, the embryo of an intercolonial business world ready to grow with the needs of the war came into existence.

Merchants on the Road to War. War came almost accidentally. A change in the East India Company Charter in 1773 allowed the company to ship tea directly to the colonies and sell it through their own agents. This, to be sure, would injure the tea business of some merchants, but the men who prevented the tea ships from unloading their cargoes were not merchants. The Whig political leaders through the Committees of Correspondence roused the Sons of Liberty. The common people of the cities, small shopkeepers, journeymen, and apprentices were the rank and file of the Sons of Liberty and of the groups that supplied popular pressure for revolution.

Only in Boston was the East India Company's tea dumped into the harbor by a raiding party and only the port of Boston was closed by the British retaliatory acts. There, where the business community was hopelessly involved in the political events, many prosperous merchants like John Hancock joined the resistance, but elsewhere the most substantial businessmen hoped to stand aloof from political strife. Insofar as merchants south of New England were represented in the Continental Congress, they generally stood for moderation and compromise. The homes of businessmen like Robert Morris of Philadelphia were meeting places for middle-of-the-road people interested in preventing a permanent break with Great Britain.

The rich have seldom been the idols of the poor, and farmers have generally distrusted the middlemen who handled supplies, but the revolutionary cleavage between lower class patriots and upper class loyalists undoubtedly added to the unpopularity of the merchants. In areas of intense patriot activity, many of the richest families thought it best to leave and entrust the protection of their property to the British government. Loyalist merchants who remained lived in fear of visits from patriot mobs bent on enforcing the nonimportation Association of 1774. (*See Reading No. 3.*)

Meanwhile, British interference with the plans of great planters, like George Washington, for buying western lands, and with the plans of common farmers, represented by Patrick Henry, for westward migration had alienated much of the population of the Old Dominion. There were no urban mobs in Virginia, since Norfolk and Williamsburg were little more than large towns, but here more than elsewhere the upper class, the important landowners, rose against British land taxes, restriction of Virginia boundaries, and the debts they owed to British merchants.

The immediate effect of Lexington and Concord in

April of 1775 was bad for all merchants. To patriot restrictions on imports or exports to Great Britain, war added the danger of capture at sea by British ships and the need for roundabout trade through neutral ports. John Hancock's business came to a standstill, although several ships dispatched in the last days of peace built his credit in London. English goods still found their way to the American market, but the volume was small, prices were high, and international payments were more difficult than usual. The result was business recession in the early years of the War, mitigated only for those able to profit from war itself.

Opportunities of the War. To those businessmen alert enough to seize them, the war offered unusual opportunities. Trades built up over two or three generations were disrupted, while new avenues to wealth opened up. Such shake-ups, never welcomed by the men involved, have been sources of new methods and occupations, of increased productivity and more efficient business operation.

Robert Morris, having reluctantly decided to support resistance, became the outstanding manipulator of wartime opportunities. With a small capital left to him by his tobacco trading father, he had executed such a smart operation in wheat that, at the age of twenty, he had been taken as a partner in an old Philadelphia firm that then became Willing and Morris. By the end of the colonial period social connections were of great commercial importance, particularly in foreign and intercolonial ventures. The Willings had supplied young Morris (he was forty-one when the war began) with a host of influential friends. Already rich and securely established, he was able quickly to reach out and organize the wartime opportunities.

British goods imported by way of the West Indies, where Willing and Morris were well served by agents, brought prices 400 per cent above those in London. Through intercolonial friendships, such as the one with Silas Deane of Hartford, Connecticut, Morris assured his house a participation in the supply of the Continental army. Deane, a member of Congress, was sent as a special agent to France and organized a syndicate for sending military supplies, carrying on English trade, and buying American lands. Morris's enthusiasm was high. To Deane he exulted: "There never has been so fair an oppert'y of making a large Fortune since I have been conversant in the World."

New trade grew rapidly with France and Holland. The fine British connections of the leading merchants were temporarily of little value; hence many merchants curtailed their overseas activities and looked for uses for their capital in manufacturing or domestic trade. Much of the new European business came into the hands of ambitious younger men like Morris who were ready to seek new continental correspondents and to learn their way around new markets.

Privateering offered another chance for high but risky wartime profit. Congress sold authorizations to prey upon British commerce, and Morris and his associates were probably the largest venturers in such auxiliary warships. That he could lose 150 ships in the course of the war and still make a profit shows the scale of his operations. It also indicates the risks involved. Many merchants had bad luck in a few privateering ventures and turned to safer activities. After France entered the war in 1778, Morris had privateers operating from French ports, and an American prize court was set up at Nantes to condemn captured vessels.

Army supply was a continual source of profit for northern merchants, particularly those in inland cities, such as Hartford, Albany, and Lancaster, where there was access to farm areas safe from British occupation. French forces paying in gold added to this market from 1779 to 1781. Jeremiah Wadsworth of Hartford became so involved in French supply that he accompanied Count Rochambeau's army to Virginia. In this way he not only assured the French of food supplies in the colonies new to them, but also increased his circle of business friends.

In the early years of the war, army quartermasters bought local supplies with state or continental currency. As paper money lost its value, the states were called on for specific kinds of supplies. But this system was cumbersome and poorly executed. Finally, in 1781, general contracts were negotiated with a small group of prosperous merchants, including some of Morris's close friends. These merchants purchased army supplies on their own credit and accepted such payments as the Continental Superintendent of Finance could arrange.

Another source of profit for those with mobile capital was the purchase of confiscated Loyalist estates. In New England and New York particularly, the estates of wealthy landowners who fled to Canada or England were confiscated by order of the Provincial Assemblies. Sales were generally at auction, and the merchants who were making money from the war were the ones who could afford to buy the best properties.

The Triumph of Business. Shortages of imported goods and consequent high prices added to the unpopularity of merchants. They were blamed for the cost of British goods and suspected of reaping enormous profits from other people's distress. "Forestallers," "regrators," and monopolizers became the public whipping boys for state and congressional politicians unable to organize adequate tax collection or army supply. A committee representing the New England states condemned "the unbounded avarice of many persons" who added to the price of the necessities of life. Even Washington wished to hang such merchants "from gallows twenty times as high as those prepared for Haman."

The solution adopted by various states between 1776 and 1780 was price fixing. Wages, commodity and service prices were set again and again, only to become meaningless as continuing issues of paper money fed the spiraling inflation. Nothing was to be had at the price fixed by law, but everything could be bought on the black market. Merchants, manufacturers, and shopkeepers opposed regulation, while men living on wages or salaries wanted prices held down. (*See Reading No. 3.*) The alignment of interests has been much the same in each period of rapid inflation

Although the Continental Congress never tried to fix prices before 1780, the anti-business, radical Whig leaders generally prevailed in national as well as state politics. From 1779 on, however, increasing prosperity, from French and British army supply and new trade, and the runaway character of the inflation, gave new strength to the mercantile interests. Congress and most of the states had virtually exhausted the power of the printing press. With new bills passing at from one mill to one cent on the dollar, there was little to be gained from further emissions. In March of 1780, Congress exchanged its paper currency for interest-bearing notes at the ratio of forty old dollars for one new and tried to arrange for new means of payment. The states also moved toward a specie basis, which meant, in fact, an increasing reliance on mercantile credit. In the spring of 1781, four Continental departments each headed by a strong leader took executive functions away from the argumentative and weak committees of Congress. The chief post of the four, recognized as such by substituting the title of Superintendent for that of Secretary, was finance, and the merchant appointed was Robert Morris. He accepted the post only on the stipulation that he could continue his private business activities.

A National Business Community. British book credit had supplied the exchange for pre-Revolutionary trade. The loss of this ultimate reserve during the war had been partly compensated by state and Continental paper money. The virtual repudiation of these currencies after 1780 again posed the problem of cash and credit resources sufficient for financing trade, and this time states freed from British restrictions were able to charter banks. As might be expected, the merchants in the main metropolitan center, Philadelphia, led the way. In 1780 they organized a nonprofit Bank of Pennsylvania, and in 1781 Robert Morris merged this into the profit-oriented Bank of North America, the world's third modern bank. Prominent merchants from as far north as Boston and Newburyport were stockholders in the Philadelphia corporation. By 1784 Boston and New York also had banks.

This new America world of finance must be seen in the light of a small, and still aristocratic country. All the states together had no more population than metropolitan Los Angeles or Philadelphia in 1950. Most men of importance must have been guests at some time in Morris's marble palace on Chestnut Street. Not only had these leaders of regional finance come to know each other through military supply and political activity during the war, but in many cases they became related by strategic marriages.

The exploitation of western lands also drew business-men and planters of the various regions together as shareholders in joint-stock companies. By 1785 the Confederation had acquired the more important state claims to the territory north of the Ohio and west of Pennsylvania. Congress was now prepared to engage in the land selling business either wholesale or retail. Powerful influences were against a government retail business. New York, Pennsylvania, and Virginia all had land for sale around the area that Congress would first open up, and they did not welcome such competition. The joint-stock companies, led by prominent citizens of many states, wanted to buy land wholesale with depreciated Continental securities and turn it over quickly at a profit. Such operations would be endangered by Congressional sales of small acreage. This combination of state and private interests explains one of the first successful attempts to keep the central government from conflicting with business. A land ordinance was passed with both minimum acreage and price set so high, and conditions of purchase so difficult, that direct sale to small farmers was virtually prevented.

With security against effective government competition, land companies successfully negotiated wholesale purchases of up to 5,000,000 acres each. The leaders of the larger companies who hoped to market land abroad as well as at home were worried by the lack of a plan of government that would provide immediate protection for settlers and their property. In 1787, Dr. Manassah Cutler, representing the Ohio Company, and William Duer, Secretary of the Board of Treasury and promoter of a new Scioto Company, joined with a number of Congressmen in working out a system of government acceptable to the land companies.

From the company standpoint the chief provision of the resulting Northwest Ordinance was that government would initially be put in the hands of a governor and three judges who could appoint other necessary officials and promulgate any of the laws of the existing states. With officials friendly to business policy, stability and order could be assured from the start. But government should also be attractive to settlers, and hence democratic procedures were to be introduced when the area reached a population of 5,000, and statehood would be the ultimate goal. That slavery was legally forbidden and education encouraged may also reflect wise business policies. At least, these businessmen inspired the Continental Congress to pass one of its few Acts of importance, one so well conceived that it remained the rule until the last mainland territory disappeared in 1959.

Business and the Constitution. Events of the 1780's emphasized the common interests of all merchants in intercolonial and foreign trade. To raise more revenue without increasing the farmer's taxes, state legislatures controlled by back-country representatives voted tariff duties. In some states, such as New York and Rhode Island, these duties soon became the chief source of revenue. Not only did they hinder trade by routing goods through customs houses with delays for inspection, but they were ultimately paid mainly by the urban residents, including the merchants themselves, who consumed large amounts of out-of-state goods. The New York legislature, dominated by up-state interests, went so far as to pass an act levying discriminatory taxes on merchants and other businessmen.

Furthermore, state tariffs stood in the way of a Continental revenue duty. The latter seemed desirable to the merchants for several reasons. It would create a free domestic market, serve as a bargaining tool in negotiating for foreign concessions, and provide Congress with money to pay off the public debt. As the initial subscribers to the state and Continental bonds used them to pay their bills, merchants had become the principal holders of public securities. Merchants accepted them at the current market rate and, when the rate was very low, such as ten or twelve cents on the dollar, some bought all they could get. Robert Morris and his New York cousin, Gouverneur, were very active in this business. Hence, the merchants came to have an interest in building governments, state and national, that were strong and conservative enough to service their debts.

The merchants were not alone in favoring a more

powerful central government. Conservatives, in general, whether landlords or businessmen, were alarmed by the strength of the small farmers in many state legislatures, and saw in an increase of national power added security against radicalism at home and enemies abroad. Presumably, the mass of the people, rural or urban, were not much interested in these problems, save as any change threatened higher internal taxes.

The movement that led to the assembling of a convention to draw up new federal articles of agreement was led by a combination of businessmen, lawyers, and planters. George Washington and James Madison, Virginia planters who wished to end interstate duties along the Potomac River, took the lead together with Alexander Hamilton, the lawyer son-in-law of the great up-state New York businessman Philip Schuyler. The Constitution drawn up at Philadelphia in 1787 was a triumph for all men who wished to safeguard private property and stimulate trade and manufactures.

Key clauses from the businessman's standpoint were those forbidding the kinds of action threatened by "radical" politicians. There could be no taxes on interstate trade, no direct federal taxes except in relation to population, no state issues of currency or interference with contracts, and no refusal to recognize the legal actions of other states. Now the national community that businessmen had been building by personal influence would have the protection of law. No longer could back-country farmer movements produce a state of near-panic in the offices of State or Chestnut Street.

Adoption of the new Constitution by conventions in nine states was accomplished only after a hard struggle with back-country representatives, but by the summer of 1788 the battle had been won without change in the original document. By 1790, with a Bill of Rights added to the Constitution, the last state had been forced into the union.

Although headed by a planter, George Washington, the new administration was in many respects a businessman's government. Washington offered Robert Morris the Secretaryship of the Treasury, and when the leading financier

declined because of the demands of his complicated
private affairs, Alexander Hamilton accepted.

Hamilton saw at long range the possibilities for American economic growth. Four policies seemed immediately
necessary: protection to encourage industry, a strong
central banking system, a revival of British investment,
and the creation of a large fund of domestic credit by
bringing the value of public securities up to par. Obviously, the latter two policies were closely allied. A
financially responsible government was an assurance to
foreign investors.

Hamilton had to settle for less than his whole program.
The very merchant interests that were his political sup-
porters bridled at really high protection, and the manufacturers who would be protected scarcely existed as a
political force. Foreign investment of all types was
drastically reduced by the outbreak of the French revolutionary wars in Europe, and British capital only became
important after the fall of Napoleon. But Congress did
establish a United States Bank with a twenty-year charter,
and enacted Hamilton's plans for raising the value of the
public debt. The latter gave a strong lift to the economy.
Not only were Continental and state certificates, formerly
worth a total of only ten or fifteen million dollars on the
market, raised in value to around sixty million dollars,
but the increase in general accrued to prosperous businessmen who would use the money for further investment in
trade and industry. For the first time there were real
security markets in New York and Philadelphia, and
money became available for turnpikes, banks, and manufacturing.

Business Meaning of the Revolution. The stirring
events from 1763 to 1791, which have been recounted
in more detail than will be accorded to any political
happenings hereafter, had greatly altered the outlook of
the businessman. He no longer looked to London as the
source of financial strength, he no longer felt powerless
to aid industrialization by favorable laws, he no longer was
barred from the West by imperial decrees, he no longer
had to smuggle to pay his debts, and he was no longer
harassed by unfriendly British officials. The businessman

of 1790 could dream of unlimited possibilities, of new industrial machinery powered by steam, of a West loaded with unexplored natural resources, of the gains possible from favorable legislation both state and national, of great capitals to be raised by means of corporations, and of maritime wealth from neutral trade among the warring nations of Europe. All the elements from which the mighty business system of the United States was to be built were now present. Putting them to work was to be a matter of the ingenuity and skill of management and the availability of competent labor.

— 4 —

THE CORPORATION

When William Duer, inspired by the far-ranging visions of Alexander Hamilton, and his Assistant Secretary of the Treasury, Tench Coxe, decided to promote manufacturing at the falls of the Passaic River in New Jersey, Duer went to Trenton and secured a corporate charter. For American businessmen of the early 1790's such procedure was becoming routine. But this was not so in the world's leading business nations, France and England. Why should this greatest of all business devices have grown up in a small nation on the edge of the wilderness?

It seems unlikely that corporations arose because of the superior acumen of American entrepreneurs. William Duer, for example, was hopelessly bankrupt by 1792, and even the great Robert Morris fell five years later. The rapid use of the corporation, 300 of which were chartered by 1800, when France and England had but a score apiece, resulted from the American situation.

Why Corporations? To begin with, business tasks, particularly in transportation, were large and the American people relatively poor. The corporation was a device for gathering moderate sums from many investors. When Duer received his New Jersey charter for the Society for Useful Manufactures, he could probably never have found an American willing to venture most of his fortune in an untried textile enterprise. But he did find dozens of substantial citizens willing to undertake a small gamble. The safest kind of stock investments appeared to be in water companies, turnpikes, and banks, but all early corporate shares had some of the aspects of lottery tickets. Four or five hundred dollars would be risked in the hope that thousands would return. The wise investor realized, or soon learned in the case of the Society for Useful Manufactures, that his stock might also become worthless.

In the matter of securing charters, the decentralization of American politics was an advantage. It was far easier to lobby a charter through a state legislature than through the British Parliament. With the wise use of money and influence, American state charters could be worded to suit the wishes of the promoters. For a few thousand dollars in payment to the state, and a few thousand more spent on Georgia legislators, Robert Morris and his associates were able to secure a charter granting the Yazoo Land Company five million acres along the Mississippi River. The Supreme Court of the United States protected such charters from alteration by later legislatures.

The corporation also enabled governments to join with private interests in subscribing for shares. Many early banks, turnpikes, and canal companies were of this "mixed type" with both public and private stockholders and directors. Looked at broadly, in such arrangements businessmen short of capital for needed improvements sought the aid of the state which could mobilize capital by use of the taxing power. (*See Reading No. 11.*)

The great optimism which accompanied national government and the promise of new means of transportation had its reverse in an intense fear in each major port that its neighbors were going to use turnpikes or canals, or, still later, railroads to draw away trade. Leading citizens equated the promotion of development corporations with local patriotism. The Philadelphia merchant was exhorted to invest in a Lancaster turnpike for fear of seeing the interior trade slip away to Baltimore. "We can and will baffle the attempts of our neighbors," proclaimed a Philadelphian. And, meanwhile, in Baltimore plans were on foot to tap the whole trade of the Ohio Valley by a great canal company. The corporation for internal improvement became a prime weapon in this regional warfare.

Corporations also suited certain American traits. They satisfied an urge to join in group activities, to solve common problems by getting together. One became a "member," became associated in the "cause" of local growth. Freely marketable shares also fitted the needs of a migratory society. The man moving from New York to Buffalo could, for example, sell his stock in the Manhattan Water Company and invest in the "patriotic" enterprises of the new city. Or, if he held stock in a promising corporation with limited liability, he might retain it, even if he could no longer observe the company's operations.

Origins of Managerial Enterprise. The business corporation was ultimately to do much more than make it easier to raise capital or to convert investments into cash: it was to create a new relationship between the ownership of property and its control. The traditional English practice of vesting control of the property in a board of directors elected annually by the stockholders was continued in America. Yet, from the earliest days in such companies as the Bank of New York the directors held but a small percentage of the stock. Of the five-hundred shares sold when the bank started its operation, the twelve directors owned only sixty-eight. These men who legally controlled the daily affairs of the bank were, therefore, operating mainly with other people's money.

The democratic procedure of an annual meeting of stockholders, somewhat like the meeting of a New England town, was required in all corporations. In the 1791 charter of the Bank of New York (*see Reading No. 4*) each share up to five owned by an individual carried one vote, but over that number the ratio decreased until above ten shares it took five to carry one vote. In theory the annual elections could have been controlled by the holders of four shares or less, but in practice this was not so. Unlike the voters at a town meeting, where everyone was somewhat informed as to what went on, the small stockholders knew very little about the affairs of the corporation. Leadership was supplied by the directors who were in possession of both the necessary information, and the machinery for reaching and influencing the stockholders. In companies with widely held stock, democracy failed from the start, and directors became a self-perpetuating group. Directorates could be overthrown, but this would be by strong financial interests buying the shares and gaining a majority of the votes at the next annual meeting, not by a revolt of the small stockholders.

Men of great wealth, who had power to gain control of a company if they so desired, often came to exercise a dominant influence on company affairs. Financiers like Nathan Appleton of Boston, called "Nathan the Wise" by his friends, used a fortune originating from trade to buy into textile mills, banks, insurance companies, and railroads. A "general entrepreneur" like Appleton sat on many boards of directors, and on important issues his desires were likely to control, even though he paid only periodic attention to the affairs of the company and owned relatively little of its stock. The few men of wealth who actively represented their interests on boards came to know each other and frequently operated in groups. Appleton was associated in his enterprises with Lowells, Cabots, Jacksons, Lees, and other families who were turning old mercantile wealth to new uses. Such loose associations of the wealthy men of Eastern Massachusetts, New York, Philadelphia, and Baltimore controlled the new corporations that had publicly marketed securities. The small stockholders quickly became passive investors whose best method of protest against bad policies was sale of their stock.

Stock Exchanges. To make stock freely transferable, it was necessary to have a meeting of brokers. Before 1790 there had been so few securities in which to trade that sales by merchants, often in coffee houses, had been the rule. But with sixty millions of funded government debt, ten million in United States bank stock and many millions more in the stocks of state banks, turn-pike, manufacturing, and land companies security trad-ing became a business in itself. In 1791 Philadelphia traders organized a stock exchange. The next year 24 New York traders agreed to deal with each other under a buttonwood tree on Wall Street. By 1794 they had moved indoors.

In these early days there was no distinction between stocks and bonds. All corporate securities were owner-ship shares, and government bonds were commonly re-ferred to as stock. Prior to the 1830's trading was seldom lively. Starting about 10:30 in the morning the name of each stock would be "called." At that time buy and sell orders would be brought forward and bidding would take place. The same process would be carried out again in the afternoon. This cumbersome practice was continued on the New York exchange until 1875.

The stock exchanges of the major cities, with New York taking the lead by 1830, were gentlemen's clubs governed only by a few house rules. No record was filed of the number of shares of company stock available for trading, no rules governed the case of the trader who could not deliver what he had sold, nothing prevented anyone from manipulating prices by buying and selling to himself through different brokers, and settlements were normally on a weekly basis. "Let the buyer beware" was the accepted rule, and conservative investors con-tinued to regard common stocks as highly speculative. In 1854, for example, Robert Schuyler, president of the New York and New Haven Railroad, printed and sold $2,000,000 worth of false stock and was safely on his way to Europe before the fraud was discovered.

Attacks on Corporations. As shown in the Schuyler case, the divorce between ownership and control, stock-holder and manager, opened new possibilities for unethical gain. Viewing the big corporations of the early 1840's, Nathan Appleton lamented: "It is a melancholy fact that there is little security for good conduct." The chief sources of danger to the stockholder were: lack of any reliable information about company activities; lack of ability to remove bad managers; and lack of assurance that man-ager's interests were the same as those of the stockholder.

This latter was the basic cause of unethical practice. Each expanding company was continually buying new property and equipment, and its president and directors might be the owners of the property bought as well as the officers of the purchaser who set the terms of sale.

Take, for example, an unprofitable branchline of railroad track. The directors of a connecting major road might quietly buy the branchline stocks and bonds at rates far below par, and then sell them at par value to the large company. If these insiders were only small stockholders in the big railroad, the effect on the value of their holdings in that company would be small, whereas the gain to themselves as the previous owners of the branchline would be large. Similar deals occurred in supplies and construction. Erastus Corning, president of the New York Central system for many years, sold his railroad all of its iron. Railroad directors formed construction companies to build their roads and in payment transferred cash and securities from the railroad which had thousands of small stockholders to the construction company largely owned by the railroads' directors. (*See Reading No. 11.*)

Speculating in company stock on the basis of advance inside information was another unethical road to wealth. By selling its stock short, as much money could be made from running a company down as from building it up.

The truly big corporation was such a new and unexplored device that management opinion against questionable practices did not begin to crystallize before the 1860's. Even the most scrupulous directors of the forties and fifties were occasionally on both sides of a bargain.

The public had long since become suspicious of the corporation. Provisions in charters for monopoly rights, for valuable franchises with no return to the government, or for the right to issue paper currency alarmed conscientious legislators and voters. The panic of 1837 with the ensuing collapse of banks in which the depositors lost their money, and of railroads that had only a few miles of graded earth to show for millions paid in by investors aroused violent anti-corporation feeling.

Stricter laws were thought to be the answer to corporate irresponsibility. One device was the general incorporation act. A standard, strictly defined charter would be estab-

lished and groups wishing to incorporate could come
under its provisions by simply paying a fee to a state
commissioner. (*See Reading No. 4.*) By 1837 such laws
were well known, but used in only a few states. Massachusetts had passed the first such act for water companies
in 1799, New York for manufacturing companies in
1811 (*see Reading No. 4*), and Michigan for banks in
1837. Where general acts existed, applications for special
chartering bills would be carefully scrutinized to see why
their sponsors did not want to use the general law. Between 1845 and 1875 the constitutions of the important
industrial states were amended to forbid special incorporation acts. In the decade following the panic of 1837,
some mid-western states prohibited all incorporation of
banks, only to relax these provisions in later years.

The Big Change. The importance of the change
from the colonial world of direct personal control of a
business to this abstract world of corporate finance where
men bought and sold property they never saw in the form
of pieces of paper, where ownership and control could
shift from day to day without in any way affecting the
conduct of company operations, can scarcely be over-
emphasized. In the old days, profit came from able
supervision of business in the course of which owners,
employees and customers met face-to-face; in the new
world of finance, money and power could accrue from
purely impersonal security manipulation. The change was
as great as that from the medieval world of feudal land-
holding and strict guild regulations to the freer world of
small-scale capitalism of the early modern period.

In discussing these early days of the corporation, the
power of directors and large financiers in relation to
small stockholders has been the major theme. In later
years, the growing power of the top-managers, those employed by the directors to run the daily affairs of the
company, was to supplant the power of directors. From
the eighteenth to the twentieth century, the migration of
effective control in large-scale corporate business has
been from operating owners to wealthy directors to professional managers.

— 5 —

THE CHALLENGE OF MANAGEMENT

There were few abler merchants than Jeremiah Wadsworth of Hartford, Connecticut. Together with Robert Morris and Alexander Hamilton, he was one of the fathers of American banking. Trained on sea voyages, as befitted all merchants, this ingratiating minister's son seized the opportunities of the Revolutionary War. After supplying the American forces he gained the contract for Count Rochambeau's army, and as we have seen (p. 33) accompanied the French forces on the final victorious campaign in Virginia. French connections brought new opportunities in trade, and Wadsworth became one of Hartford's wealthiest citizens. Meanwhile, he had interested himself in Morris's Bank of North America. He sold its stock to men in Connecticut, not an easy task in the case of this pioneer venture; he also kept 104 shares, the largest single holding, for himself. In 1784 he joined with a former partner, John Barker Church, and with Alexander Hamilton in promoting the Bank of New York. In the early nineties Wadsworth had the eloquent Peleg Sanford, one of his clerks, convince a meeting of local businessmen of the need for a Hartford Bank. Having seen to the establishment of this business, Wadsworth turned with equal success to marine insurance.

Thus, in the early days of the Republic, the great traders of the Revolutionary period like Morris and Wadsworth continued to be the big operators in new fields, whereas, after 1800, merchants like John Jacob Astor and Stephen Girard expanded their activities to win even larger fortunes than the older generation had ever known. Astor made millions in furs and real estate as well as in the China trade, and Girard put profits from European voyages into real estate, insurance, and banking. Other merchants, such as Francis Cabot Lowell, Amos Lawrence and Nathan Appleton, built the textile industry of Massachusetts.

Early Bank Management.   Merchants not only supplied capital for the rapid rise of banking after the Revolution, and of manufacturing after 1800, but most of the management as well. Each new activity, such as banking, challenged the ingenuity of the men of the counting house. There were no books dealing with American conditions, no consultants to hire, no attorneys versed in banking law. Each bank had to proceed on a trial-and-error basis, and there was plenty of error.

The boards of directors of the early banks acted as the management. The president was simply the board's chairman. The cashier, who was ultimately to become the operating manager, initially had little freedom of action. The board meeting held once or twice a week passed on each individual loan or discount and authorized each investment in securities. Without much regard for the policies of England, France, or Holland, these metropolitan merchants and lawyers laid the foundations of American banking.

One question after another had to be decided, first by the Bank of North America in Philadelphia (1782), then by the New York and Massachusetts banks (1784), and soon by a dozen banks in smaller cities. Building upon each other's experience, they developed fairly uniform policies. In accordance with the practice of the government loan offices of the colonies, they made their loans in circulating currency—engraved notes of fixed value with some distinctive picture on the face—rather than by creating deposits or issuing drafts. Save in the case of other banks, overdrafts, a British system of lending by allowing the borrower to write a check for more than his deposits, were not approved. No one knew exactly how much it was safe to lend. Some banks lent 100 per cent of their capital and deposits, some two or three times their capital, the conservative Hartford Bank limited loans to two thirds of deposits.

As the business of the bank grew in size and complexity it needed the full attention of professional managers. At first the board of directors tried to meet the situation by forming special committees for different functions, but by the 1820's the business of big banks was too much for any outside directors to administer. Also, some paper came to require faster action than a semi-weekly meeting of the board. The result was transference of control over daily transactions to the cashier and the appointment of a working president who could make decisions between directors meetings. While inevitably divorcing directors from intimate knowledge of the affairs of their bank, the new arrangements assured depositors and borrowers of more secrecy. These changes, portentous of what was to happen in all big business, did not occur everywhere at once. As early as 1824, Nicholas Biddle, a strong-minded president, was running the Second Bank of the United States pretty much to suit his own ideas, whereas in some country banks active administration by directors lasted throughout the first half of the century.

Early Banking Problems.   The big city institutions were businessmen's banks. Their shares, valued at four or five hundred dollars each, kept ownership in the hands of prosperous merchants and lawyers. They made no appeals for small deposits. In fact, the Massachusetts bank for a time charged the depositors a fee. The boards preferred to make thirty- or sixty-day loans on paper representing goods in transit or ready for sale. (*See Reading No. 5.*)

But American conditions in general were against such conservative "money banks." The businessmen of the young Republic wanted credit for expansion, and they wanted banks to create the credit. By the nineties accommodation paper was taking its place beside "real" commercial paper even in the portfolios of the metropolitan banks. Accommodation meant a note signed by the borrower and endorsed by a man of substance, promising to pay in ninety days. If security was given, it was likely to be in mortgages or stocks. The borrower generally used the proceeds of the loan for more working capital or expansion of his operations. Hence, at the end of each ninety days he asked for and customarily received a renewal. As Mathew Carey, the early economist, saw it in 1807, the money borrowed from the First Bank of the United States had been sunk in houses, factories, and ships, in places, that is, from which money could not be immediately recovered.

This was good for the growth of the nation, but dangerous to the lending bank. The big city banks could keep a high percentage of truly self-liquidating paper, but the portfolios of the country banks that financed farmers and other small enterprises became stocked with accommodation paper that could only be collected gradually, if at all. As a result, when the trade embargoes and the War of 1812 brought hard times, the country banks had to suspend payment of their circulating notes. It is easy to say that the situation showed the ignorance and incompetence of early bankers. But in the American back country it was hard to support a bank on any other basis. The issue was shaky banks or none at all, and until the dire panic of 1837 most communities preferred to have weak banks and more credit.

To facilitate inter-city payments banks deposited with each other, and occasionally borrowed as well. Even conservative boards authorized loans to governments, secured by government "stocks," and the purchase of stocks of canal, bridge, and turnpike companies.

The errors of early American banking came not only from failure to understand that deposits were a liability similar to printed notes, or that renewed loans were not sufficiently liquid, but also from a lack of proper ethics. Merchant directors often permitted each other to pay for their stock, the bank's capital, with promissory notes. They and their friends might then become the chief borrowers. Sometimes loans were granted to build up a political party.

Between 1800 and 1837 too many banks were operated chiefly for the purpose of issuing paper currency in loans at high interest rates and dividing the profits among directors who had paid in no cash. As early as 1809,

Timothy Dexter, Jr., provided a classic example of the process. He and a few friends bought control of a Glocester, Rhode Island, bank with promissory notes. The bank never had more than a few hundred dollars in real money, and its cashier spent most of his time shut up in a back room signing bank notes of small denominations which were then lent as far as possible fom Glocester. Some notes even reached Ohio, but their main area of circulation was western Massachusetts where Dexter owned similar banks. By 1809, with some $800,000 in notes outstanding it was no longer possible to keep up the pretense of redemption and the banking office closed. Other dishonest "bankers" made the place for redemption of notes a remote cabin in a place populated only by forest animals—hence the term "wildcat" currency.

Protection of the public against fraudulent or reckless bankers gave American businessmen one of their first problems in the limits of free enterprise as against state regulation. The solution always most acceptable to businessmen was self-regulation. To a degree this was accomplished in New England by the Suffolk Bank of Boston. This bank went into the business of collecting country bank notes for other Boston banks. This in turn led to country bank deposits with the Suffolk Bank and to a "clearing" of the various bank's claims against each other by transfers at the Suffolk. Through this process, similar to the formally organized clearing houses of the 1850's, the Suffolk Bank could police the notes of weak banks and threaten massive demands for note redemption if they thought a particular bank was overissuing. (See Reading No. 5.) The First and Second Banks of the United States (1791-1811 and 1816-1836) exercised a somewhat similar restraint over excessive note issues.

However, the regulation of banking by bankers was not sufficient. State laws were passed in the 1820's and 1830's providing for reserves of state bonds against bank notes, limiting circulation in relation to capital, and in some instances establishing "safety funds" contributed to by all the banks to protect bank currency. Legal safeguards were made even more necessary as Michigan in 1837, followed by New York in 1838, set the example of "free" banking. In the states with such laws, an entrepreneur could incorporate a bank as easily as any other enterprise and start issuing notes, subject to state regulations.

The panic of 1837 which had dire effects on hundreds of small banks, and a few of the larger ones, led to a strong wave of anti-bank feeling that further weakened the business organization of banking. During the next dozen years several states in the West and Southwest prohibited the chartering of banks. Such laws proved ineffective for curing the evils of bad management and weak notes. With no legal banknotes of their own the prohibiting states became lush grounds for the circulation of all sorts of out-of-state currency issued by both chartered banks and private individuals. By mid-century the bank currency situation was in confusion and "exchange" (notes that would be accepted) from one city on another was nearly as difficult to arrange as in international trade. Localism and fear of big corporations had triumphed over advancing European ideas of central and branch banking.

Manufacturing. Although private banking of a sort had been practiced by most large merchants and the physical aspects of bank management were much like those of a mercantile office, factory operation opened a new world. Technology had to be understood by men who had never before used machines. Labor had to be recruited and disciplined work schedules maintained, costs reckoned, and customers found for the product. The co-ordination of all these activities presented a stern test of management and most early entrepreneurs failed to pass.

Manufacturing was, as the reader knows, already the occupation of many Americans. Saw, grist, and rolling mills used the power of countless streams, forges processed the numerous surface deposits of iron ore, every town and city had home workshops supplying local customers; but factory industry, mass production involving scores of workers in one building, was something new. As in most countries, the earliest factories were spinning mills. By the 1780's Americans could build spinning machinery similar to English models. But prior to 1800 most efforts failed from lack of worker and managerial know-how In the one case of outstanding success an experienced

British textile mechanic, Samuel Slater, became the plant manager for a firm of shrewd Providence merchants, Almy and Brown. (*See Reading No. 6.*)

To convert a man or woman conditioned to the rhythms of the farm and unfamiliar with any machinery more complicated than a wringer into a machine tender from dawn until dark had been universally difficult and the United States was no exception. Machinery broke from careless operation, absenteeism and quitting the job were common, and the role of the foreman was not understood. Although these problems could be mastered through patient training by the owner of the mill or a good superintendent, the lack of mechanics who could tend and repair machinery and supervise operations remained acute until the 1830's, when a new generation had arisen familiar from youth with machines.

The scheduling of production was further complicated by the fact that most early processes were a combination of machine work in the factory and hand operations put-out to neighboring farmers. Production of thread, for example, began by baled cotton being delivered to farmers who served the mill. For a fee of four to six cents a pound they picked the cotton apart and whipped it free of impurities. Then the mill wagon collected the cotton for carding, drawing, and spinning by machinery. The thread was sold largely to city merchants, but some was kept in the community for home weaving.

Who were these early entrepreneurs who dared risk their money in such uncertain ventures? Usually they were men who had some experience with either the product or the machinery. Merchants who marketed thread or cloth associated themselves with mechanics who claimed to know mill machinery. Blacksmiths, who at this period made and repaired all sorts of devices, were not afraid to try a venture in a nearby machine-run mill. Gunsmiths built or imported lathes, and turned to machine-made hardware. Eli Whitney and Simeon North progressed toward making guns of mass-produced interchangeable parts.

Skilled handicraft workers who shifted to machinery were likely to overemphasize production and neglect accounting and marketing. Often the proprietors used up much of their time adjusting machines, guiding workers, and doing other things that should have been tended to by a foreman or superintendent. They were averse to spending money to hire someone who could do Italian (double entry) bookkeeping, but quite unable to keep good books themselves. A partner was usually found to tend to selling, which meant trips to the nearby cities to establish contacts.

In all firms, particularly those managed by three or four brothers, there was also likely to be poor definition of authority and consequent friction. When one of these owner-managers saw something being done wrong, he was likely to issue an order without regard for the fact that the operation did not fall in his province of management. In spite of family cooperation, however, a present-day businessman looking at almost any manufacturing concern of the first half of the nineteenth century probably would say that it was undermanaged.

In the period from 1800 to 1830 it is impossible to judge whether poor allocation of managerial duties or lack of capital was the most important cause of failure in manufacturing. These causes usually worked together, and have continued hand in hand to the present day. The ambitious men of each town with a fast flowing stream sought to start some kind of manufacture. They had energy, ingenuity, and were willing to work hard, but almost invariably they lacked experience and money. The textile mills that made large profits were the well-equipped plants founded by rich merchants of the coast cities like the Boston Manufacturing Company of the Lowells, Jacksons, and Appletons. Those that failed were the scores of back-country spinning mills capitalized at thirty dollars a spindle in borrowed money. (*See Reading No. 6.*)

Back-country failure was by no means universal. Four of the five sons of blacksmith Paul Whitin of North-bridge, Massachusetts, teamed together to run first a successful spinning mill and later a textile machinery plant. But two things bear out our general conclusion: John Whitin, one of the brothers, had spent the greater part of his youth learning about textile machinery and, although the Whitins were succeeding, nearly every nearby mill failed and suspended operations.

The need for economy in men both laboring and managerial made the American factory system different from that of Europe from the beginning. The high cost of labor encouraged the use of machines, and more mechanization permitted higher wages. As a result, by 1850 mechanization with its aim of interchangeable parts was called in England "the American system." (*See Reading No. 6.*)

Once American management secured men with the necessary skills, the social system and the general culture also contributed strongly to efficient operation. Young American workers were not afraid to think for themselves. Most managers had no social status that made them feel superior to their employees. The latter expected to get ahead and soon to be owners or managers themselves. The combination made for a drive and emphasis on productivity in American plants that surprised visiting Europeans. (*See Reading No. 6.*) Thus, early industrial management developed productive efficiency, measured in labor, and was mechanically innovative, while its paperwork and market adjustments remained crude.

The Business Cycle. A poorly run factory with inadequate working capital, no reserves for depreciation and uncertain trade connections, that just struggled along in prosperous years, could not survive prolonged depression. Before the 1820's, depressions were not anticipated. Until after the War of 1812, ups and downs of economic activity had always appeared to be influenced more by European trade and crop conditions than any local business factors. After the panic of 1819, however, perceptive entrepreneurs began to recognize a cycle of ups and downs dependent on American as well as English business expectations.

The opinion of men of the day as well as most later observers was that the sharp breaks in American prosperity, such as 1819, 1837, and 1857, were caused by prolonged periods of overinvestment. Canals up to 1837, railroads in the later years and western lands perennially were the speculative favorites. In years of great optimism, money committed to such development exceeded the savings of the nation and caused inflationary spirals in wages, prices, and interest rates. Eventually, the wiser financiers would become alarmed. "I don't like to take hold of things when at too high a tide," wrote railroad financier John Murray Forbes just before the minor recession of 1847. As they and their friends abstained from further commitments the stock market would break, sometimes in panic, if the boom had been big, at other times in orderly but prolonged declines.

The businessman was then hit by banks asking for the reduction of loans, hitherto renewed, whose proceeds were tied up in working capital. Orders were canceled, and potential customers held off to buy their goods at distress sales. There was nothing to do but close the shop. The bank, in turn, failed to get the money needed to pay off scared depositors and note holders, and likely there was nothing to do but close the bank. These closings were not permanent. When times became better, the old proprietors or new owners who had bought the bankrupt concerns started up again, but American business life was more uncertain, more subject to ups and downs, to waves of blind optimism and unrelieved pessimism, than that of other countries. In the form of an exaggerated business cycle, America paid periodic penalties for its precocious rate of advance. Those entrepreneurs who started their firms early in the periods between major depressions might be strong enough to weather the storm when it came; those whose firms were still in the shoe-string stage of finance when depressions hit were forced to close down or sell out to stronger competitors.

In America, however, failure has never been taken seriously. Most businessmen started with very little capital and, if it was lost, the erstwhile proprietor worked for someone else until he had saved enough to try again. R. H. Macy failed several times in smaller places before he succeeded in New York. Successful firms like Reed and Barton had early histories of closings, reopenings, failures, and changes in ownership. The entrepreneurial vigor created by American resources and American culture has been demonstrated not in unusual acumen or an extraordinary ratio of success to failure, but in a persistent quest for profit-making enterprise.

Business Organizes. Forming associations to consider business problems was another American pattern. Colonial handicraftsmen had had city-wide associations; even the nonimportation agreements of pre-Revolutionary days may be seen as a form of business association. In the young Republic, cities and states formed associations to promote manufacturing. By 1820 manufacturers, such as E. I. duPont and Peter Colt, formed the National Institution for the Promotion of Industry to lobby for a higher tariff.

In the years after the War of 1812 river steamboat operators were in such cutthroat competition that they were forced to form associations on the Ohio and the North Rivers to control rates and service. But regional trade associations did not spread in this period. (*See Reading No. 6.*) Associations of employers, however, were formed on a local basis to deal with labor relations and keep unions out of the new factories.

Beside the interest of manufacturers in tariff protection, many businessmen wanted special incorporation laws, and canal and railroad promoters needed franchises and financial aid from government. Having received special privileges, these companies often had to defend them in later legislative sessions. The result was the evolution of the lobbyist or legislative councilor. Usually he was a lawyer who practiced in Washington or one of the state capitals, and knew the key men in party and legislature. As early as 1816 Theron Rudd performed such services for John Jacob Astor, Stephen Girard, and others in steering a charter through Congress for the Second Bank of the United States.

Railroad and canal companies lobbied for state and local subscription to their stock and bonds as well as monopoly privileges. Like some of the banks, a number of these companies became "mixed" enterprises in which the state owned stock and elected directors. During these years the ideas regarding the separation of government and business had not yet crystallized, and both sides joined without much regard to "principles" in promoting the economic development of their region by whatever means seemed practical.

The Business Scene. In addition to large resources

and a favorable cultural tradition, early American business benefited from both domestic and foreign migration. The newcomer to a community brought ideas and practices from other areas. He was in general a young man of more than average ability, and he worked hard to fit into his adopted community. Foreigners, particularly, brought both capital and skills to American business. German brewers, Welsh iron masters, and English mechanics, for example, brought highly developed Old-World techniques. They also brought ideas of trade union organization.

While the rapid development of banking and manufacturing introduced new challenges to management, the great majority of businessmen, those in trade and service, continued to operate much as before. Some merchants in the biggest ports found it profitable for several decades to sell many imported goods at auction. Specialized jobbers and brokers increased in number, but one familiar with the mercantile world of 1790 would not have had difficulty in adjusting to that of 1850. The general store had carried the habits of trade and business calculation to the most remote frontiers, but it was still the same cluttered room full of butter kegs and cheeses, dresses and farm implements, cracker and whiskey barrels. A few lines of railroad track connected the big cities of the East, passenger steamers had replaced the sailing ship, the telegraph had just reached the West, but the pace of business was still slow. Inland customers still came in person spring and fall to buy at the metropolitan wholesale centers, credit terms were still geared to a six months' rhythm. The business world inherited from the colonial days was considerably altered, but the biggest changes were still to come.

— 6 —

A NATION-WIDE MARKET

In 1850 groups of Boston, New York, and Philadelphia financiers were racing each other to see whose railroad would first connect at Chicago with lines fanning out toward the South and West. Eventually all the financiers won, for there was soon enough business to keep each East-West trunkline busy. The spread of the continuous railroad net in the fifties to include LaCrosse, Wisconsin, on the Upper Mississippi, St. Joseph on the northward bend of the Missouri, and New Orleans and Mobile on the Gulf opened a national market.

By 1890 the market had grown from 25 to over 60 million consumers. This continental market together with great resources in coal, iron, copper, oil, timber, farming land, and technology challenged business leaders as never before. The heroic figures of the age like Carnegie, Hill, Rockefeller, or Vanderbilt, by ably exploiting the major opportunities, profited fabulously and built bigger companies than the world had ever seen. Most of these men began in one of the older businesses and then shifted to the new pursuits at an opportune time. Both Hill and Rockefeller were merchants before Hill went into railroads and Rockefeller into oil. Vanderbilt was a ferryman in New York harbor, and ultimately an important steamship owner before shifting to railroads. Of the group named, only Carnegie was, from the start, a continuously opportunistic operator, playing all the possibilities opened by his quick mind, magnetic personality, and soft Scotch burr. While his great ultimate commitment was to steel, he made money in railroads, Pullman cars, and half a dozen other things on the way up.

Civil War delayed the nation's great physical growth for a few years, but in the long run its effects were stimulating. While it checked railroad building, factory construction, and immigration, it put money in the hands of northern businessmen and, by inflation, reduced the relative size of old debts, such as railroad bonds. Few of the great business leaders became involved in the war except through supply contracts.

factors

The Pressures of Competition. Ironically, two of the three factors that were making American enterprise great on a world scale harassed the local businessman. In many lines of manufacture ever cheaper railroad rates put everyone in the nation in competition with each other, and the increasing productivity of industrial machinery continuously threatened overproduction and gave an advantage to the company with the newest machines. A third factor, generally declining prices from 1865 to 1897, put pressure on all businessmen to keep down inventories and speed turnover.

Added to these pressures was the increasing violence of the business cycle. Following the panic of 1857 there was no real recovery before secession. Not until the spring of 1863 were war orders and labor shortages sufficient to improve conditions in the prostrate Middle-West. Again, from 1873 until 1879, and from 1883 to 1886, business stagnated in depressions. The result of all these factors, cheap transportation, overproduction, price declines, and depressions, was a period of the most difficult competition that modern business has gone through, one often referred to in Europe simply as "the great depression."

Paradoxically, it was a period of great increases in capital and productivity: a period in which competitive problems harassed the businessman, but benefited the consumer; one in which the salaried middle class and the skilled workers became more prosperous and increasingly conscious of the "American standard of living."

The first form of relief sought by manufacturers made desperate by price cuts was usually an association of the principal producers to try to restrict output and regulate prices. In England and continental Europe such associations or cartels succeeded, but in the United States there were legal difficulties. The state courts interpreted the common law so that agreements to raise prices and restrict production were criminal conspiracies. Consequently, such inter-company arrangements had to be "gentlemen's agreements" rather than legally binding contracts, and no industry was completely run by gentlemen. (*See Reading No. 8.*)

The troubles of the whiskey distillers north of the Ohio River illustrated the difficulties of reaching any stable arrangement short of a unified combination or trust. In the 1870's internal revenue taxes and consequent decline in the use of industrial alcohol left the distillers with large excess capacity. They tried to quota production at two fifths, but the agreement failed to hold. "Our experience," said one of them, "was that a distiller would keep on until all his own money and all he could borrow was gone, and when he was used up there was another man ready to step in his shoes." Desperate by 1881 the distillers formed an export pool. Each one had a quota and beyond this his whiskey was to be turned over to the pool to sell abroad at less than domestic prices. To finance the pool, each firm paid an assessment based on its consumption of grain. The first pool lasted barely six months before a member refused to pay his assessment —and legal compulsion was, of course, impossible. And so year after year agreements were solemnly made, sometimes for restriction to as little as 25 per cent of capacity, only to be broken when it was to someone's advantage.

By the spring of 1887 the leaders were convinced that no pool or agreement could hold, and the meeting of that year proposed a trust, modeled after Standard Oil. Each distillery was generously appraised, and the owners received the amount in $100 certificates of trust. The combined plants would be administered by nine elected trustees, just as directors run an ordinary corporation. The economic advantage of such a combination over a cartel or association that would have kept everyone in business is indicated by the fact that, of more than eighty distilleries turned over to the trust, the twelve most efficient proved adequate to supply all the whiskey that could be sold.

Such was the voluntary road to bigger, more efficient business, one that has been continuously followed from that day to this. Most such consolidations have not produced monopolies, any more than in the case of the distillers trust, but they have served to eliminate inefficient, cutthroat competition. Aside from the few instances in which monopoly resulted, the greatest weakness in these early mergers was overcapitalization. After the properties involved had been assessed at very high rates, additional trust certificates were sold to the public to raise money for improvements and working capital, while further large blocks of certificates were given as a commission to the investment banking house that sold the securities. As a result, the trust might start in business with a capitalization twice as high as the total of the former independent companies.

A more spectacular road to bigness was conquest of a large share of the market and elimination of weaker competitors by one big company. Carnegie Steel illustrates this type of growth. Driven by the relentless Andrew Carnegie, the company was so much more efficient than its competitors, and soon had so much bigger volume, that small mills could not compete in rails, structural steel, or heavy plate.

Standard Oil was a combination of company growth and mergers. Efficient, well-located competitors were invited to bring their refineries into the combine on favorable terms and become officers, less efficient refiners were forced to come in on unfavorable terms, or were bought out for cash at distress prices. John D. Rockefeller was the leader from the beginning and until he ceased going to the office in 1899, but he never ruled by force. Unlike Carnegie in steel, he never held a majority of the stock, and Standard was guided by group decisions which Rockefeller influenced through business wisdom. (*See Reading No. 12.*)

The remaining road to corporate bigness was through purchase of the stock of companies in the open market. Since prior to 1890 few industrial firms had stock that was listed on security exchanges, this method applied chiefly to railroads. By it Vanderbilt, Villard, Huntington, Stanford, Gould, and many others built up large railroad combinations. By the end of the century, half a dozen groups of owners associated through banking houses controlled most of the important mainline network. This worked for economic efficiency in management, connections, and use of equipment, but threatened the shipper with noncompetitive service and rates, and hence led to increasingly strict government regulation. (*See Reading No. 11.*)

Managing Big Business.   Aside from the pressures of competition, supplying a nation-wide market made for bigger multi-plant companies in many lines of business. This, in turn, brought new problems in management. When Francis Cabot Lowell organized the first complete textile factory at Waltham, Massachusetts, in 1814, he had to cope with recruiting and disciplining of labor, training supervisors, scheduling production, keeping accounts, and selling. But all the plant operations were at Waltham, and selling involved just one exclusive contract with B. C. Ward and Company in nearby Boston. He had to justify his actions to a board of directors composed of relatives and close friends. When Charles E. Perkins became president of the Chicago, Burlington & Quincy Railroad in 1881, most of the challenges that Lowell and fellow manager, P. T. Jackson, had struggled with at Waltham were now routine operations, but new problems much larger and more complex had taken their place. Perkins's organization stretched from a head office in Boston to divisional organizations close to the Rocky Mountains. The road's long-run policies were set at directors meetings in Boston, while operating control was in Chicago. Dozens of middle managers of all types had to make decisions that would coordinate the system. Accounting had to be used as a control over efficiency as well as a means of balancing books. Selling the service meant relations with hundreds of thousands of customers and with many units of government. It is not surprising that railroad executives led the way in learning how to manage big companies.

Basically, the problem of top management is one of communication, of knowing what is going on and transmitting proper instructions to the people who do the actual work. By the 1850's accounting was recognized as one of the best ways of knowing what was going on. President Brooks of the Michigan Central Railroad instructed his auditor in 1859 to examine "in detail into the manner in which the work of the various departments of expenditure is executed . . . to the end that (without impairing efficiency) the number of employees may be reduced and the most economical result be attained." Cost accounting was attempted in industry and transportation, but usually by means which were not very satisfactory or revealing. Replacements were charged as current expenses rather than planned for through depreciation accounts. But without accounting, even in its crude form, the control of big multi-plant companies would have been impossible.

In the early mills, supervisors saw the boss almost daily and discussed all kinds of problems with him. In big companies such informality was impossible. By the 1870's communication was "bureaucratized." Each man had to send information upward through his immediate superior, and he received orders through the same chain of command. "The Company" became an impersonal entity, a sort of Holy Ghost, that communicated with the employee only in writing or through his supervisor.

How to preserve efficiency and good morale under these new conditions troubled every thoughtful executive. Furthermore, the top officers busy with finance and marketing might lack the knowledge necessary for exact supervision of complex technology. Inside contracting was one solution. In 1854, Henry V. Poor recommended in his *American Railroad Journal* that all the operations of the roads be let out on contract.

Although construction was almost invariably by contract, railroads never pushed inside contracting as far as some other big companies. Winchester Repeating Arms, for example, had about half the employees in its gun shop working for contractors. The contractor was a foreman who hired his own workers but used the company shop and its machines. He was charged for materials and other supplies and delivered the finished products to the company at a fixed price. While he could make a profit by efficient operation, he was guaranteed a foreman's daily wage. The practice flourished wherever complicated operations were involved. R. H. Macy's early department store in New York had several departments run by contract. (*See Reading No. 8.*)

When direct introduction of the personal profit motive was not considered feasible, delegation of authority and responsibility might serve the same purpose. "It is obvious," said President Perkins, "that to hold a manager responsible for the results it is necessary to give him pretty full power over the property which he must use to produce these results, both as to income and outgo." Thus, during the nineteenth century the old system of local personal operation existed in the big company side by side with the new system of centralized control.

Along with the growing size of the managerial hierarchy and delegation of authority came new titles. "Superintendents" became subordinate to "general superintendents," and they in turn to "managers" and "general managers." First, second, third, and fourth vice-presidents were created, and then numbering was abandoned for functional titles such as "Vice-President for Sales." Outside professionals who gave advice on law, engineering, or science were made a part of salaried management. The railroads, for example, quickly hired full-time lawyers and their work developed into legal departments headed by vice-presidents. In the 1870's Andrew Carnegie claimed that he was the first steel man to put a German university trained chemist on his regular staff.

All this evolution in the structure of management came from experience. There were no business schools on the college level before the Wharton School of the University of Pennsylvania in 1884 and no textbooks specializing on marketing or management. Some trade papers, such as Poor's *American Railroad Journal,* carried occasional articles recounting the experience of various firms and offering suggestions, but it does not appear that practical managers took many ideas directly from such sources. Rather, innovations came from meeting situations and by a grapevine of conversation and letters. Managerial concepts grew faster, therefore, in an area like railroading, where hundreds of managers faced common problems, than in more specialized operations, such as arms manufacture.

Managers and Owners. As management grew to be a substantial group of trained, intelligent men with aims and principles of their own, its relations to the stockholders and directors became more complex. In the beginning, John Murray Forbes thought that running the Michigan Central Railroad would be a part-time job that he could attend to in spare evenings at home in Massachusetts. He soon learned that directors who could not devote a great deal of time to the affairs of a big company could know very little about what went on. They had to rely for information on the full-time salaried officers. This meant that more officers were added to the board of directors. The presidents had almost always been members, but now treasurers and some vice-presidents took seats, and the chairmanship of the board became in some companies a salaried job.

Up to 1890, most of the boards of the big companies were still dominated in matters of ultimate policy by important stock-owning financiers. Four or five such men, often from the same area, and occasionally relatives, could in a showdown marshal the votes of a majority of the stockholders. Seeing the company from their position as owners, these important capitalists might truly represent the absent stockholders, but on occasion influential directors saw the company as a property to be manipulated for their personal benefit.

Prior to the Civil War, the relations of trusteeship were not clear. As noted in Chapter 4, honorable directors saw nothing amiss in being on both sides of bargains: in selling their railroads iron that they as merchants had imported; in authorizing contracts with construction companies that they owned; in buying land from the company at low prices and reselling at high; or in owning bridges or grain elevators that a railroad used. In the case of railroads, many of the bad practices existed because of the scarcity of capital, and charter restrictions on the conditions of sale of securities. If, as was often the case, the charter stipulated that the railroad stock could only be sold initially at par, it might become unsalable in the open market. But the large capitalists connected with the road could form a construction company that would lay the track at high prices and take stock at par in payment. Or, it might be that when the track was completed the railroad lacked capital for essential facilities, such as grain elevators or stockyards. Here again, the capitalist directors would come forward with a separate company to supply the need.

As has so often been the case, more comfortable financial circumstances and higher ethics went hand in hand. In Boston, where capital for sound ventures was relatively plentiful, corporate practices became strictly defined; in Dubuque, Iowa, where capital for any purpose was scarce, corporate directors remained opportunists. By the 1880's the successful, well-managed railroads had developed the code of ethics concerning stockholders and directors that was to appear adequate until 1929. "The smallest kind of interest in a coal mine," wrote President Perkins to a top officer of the Burlington system, "would be objectionable." He went on to condemn officers who "make money out of side shows." Directors' relations to the general public remained undefined, particularly in industrial companies, but there was general understanding of directors obligations to stockholders, even if such obligations were not always respected. (*See Reading No. 12.*)

Selling in a National Market.   The peddler on a horse with saddle bags full of clocks and knives and other light manufactures was the forerunner of the traveling salesman. He brought some of the material civilization and the talk of the East to the most remote frontier. Often a New Englander by origin, he created a myth of Yankee sharpness. But the general storekeeper was seldom far behind the peddler. Some frontier farmer would start a grist mill or begin to carry a few articles and soon he would be in general trade bringing in the goods his neighbors wanted. Furthermore, his store would become a community center, a sort of library, fashion mart, open forum, and tavern all in one. Abraham Lincoln and thousands of other young frontiersmen received their principal education in American ways at a nearby general store. (*See Reading No. 7.*)

The storekeeper had to make tedious and often dangerous journeys to visit big city wholesalers about twice a year to replenish his stock. The spread of the railroad after 1850 began to change this practice. Now the larger, more enterprising producers started to send salesmen out on the road to visit wholesalers and retailers. The traveler telegraphed the orders that needed to be filled quickly, and his company shipped by one of the new express companies. As this method of selling became the rule, the ubiquitous salesman with his sample case and order book, his jokes and tall stories, his proclivities as a man away from home, became a symbol of American business.

Nation-wide distribution of factory products, including packaged cereals and other branded foods, led to new wholesalers and jobbers in each distributing center. Factory salesmen visited wholesalers, who bought their goods, and brokers or jobbers who sold mainly on commission. These firms, in turn, sent their salesmen to the retailers within their area. Occasionally, factory salesmen reinforced these efforts by visiting the larger retailers. The marketing structure reached its maximum degree of complexity by the end of the nineteenth century. Wheat, for example, passed through the hands of so many middlemen, before reaching the consumer, that farmers claimed they received only a small fraction of the retail price.

Selling at a distance on credit with no more knowledge of the character of a local retailer than could be picked up by a fast-moving traveling salesman could be a risky business. The panic of 1837 and the ensuing series of bankruptcies illustrated how great the risk was. To supply reliable information on men all over the United States, Lewis Tappan in 1841 organized the Mercantile Credit Agency, later to be known as R. G. Dun & Co. In 1849 John M. Bradstreet started competition that continued until these two pioneer credit agencies merged in 1933.

As the tempo of supply became geared to railway express schedules and stock could be turned over several times a year, credit terms became shorter. The old six-month or even annual settlement was replaced by sixty or ninety days with discounts for quicker payments. The catalogue or salesman's sample took the place of journeys to the selling centers. Nation-wide advertising in local papers began to pay.

Advertising, in the form of notices of goods received

from abroad, of a craftsman's products, or of a new store or tavern was as old as the first newspapers. By the early nineteenth century many more newspapers carried many more advertisements, but the advertisers were still local and the type of notice had scarcely changed. The cost of rag paper and the difficulty of printing many pages on a flat-bed press led publishers to restrict the size of advertisements. Pictorial display was prohibited or discouraged. The numerous magazines, each with a very small circulation, carried little but book advertising.

Between 1845 and 1870 changes in technology completely altered the relationship of advertisers to their media. In the late forties the rotary press made it easy to print large editions. By the late sixties the sulfite process substituted plentiful wood pulp for scarce rags in papermaking. Meanwhile, the railroad opened a national market for both media and products, and special agencies appeared to place advertising.

Until about 1890 newspapers, daily and weekly, remained the chief media. Many weeklies were religious publications with wide circulation. Patent medicines accounted for so much of the national advertising that advertising filler supplied by news agencies to local papers was called "patent insides." To know all these papers and what they were worth to different types of advertisers was the main task of the early agencies.

In 1879, N. W. Ayer & Son of Philadelphia made a market analysis of newspapers for a threshing machine manufacturer. On the basis of this pioneering work they landed the contract that was worth the great sum of $18,000 for the next year. Soon Ayer and the other agencies were giving advice on copy, supplying artists, and planning campaigns. But, in spite of a few firms like the makers of Sapolio or Eastman Kodak that spent hundreds of thousands annually, advertising before the end of the 1880's remained small-scale. Many firms thought it beneath their dignity to advertise in cheap newspapers; still more doubted that it would pay.

Finance. By the Civil War it was obvious that a currency system in which each state or private bank issued its own paper notes, acceptable in distant cities only at a discount, could not serve the purposes of nation-wide business. Alongside the thousands of legitimate notes, identifiable only by experts, circulated thousands of counterfeits. No one would accept strange currency until it had been carefully identified and evaluated. It is reported that there was a day in the panic-stricken fall of 1857 when no money that would pass in New York was available in the city of Chicago.

To correct this chaotic situation, made worse by secession, and to help finance the Civil War, a national banking system was established in 1863. Two years later state banknotes were taxed out of existence. The nation now had a paper currency made up of the uniformly engraved notes of national banks, secured by federal bonds, and of a limited amount of government greenbacks and silver and gold certificates. (*See Reading No. 9.*)

The National Banking Act provided a workable solution to the currency problem, but did not greatly improve the business structure of banking. In the postwar years, businessmen learned that checks could do almost all the work of printed notes. Consequently, most local bankers preferred the freedom of operation permitted under a state charter or no charter to the more rigorous rules and inspections of the national system. In 1890 there were 4,700 state chartered and unchartered banks as against 3,500 in the national system, and the number of banks outside the system was growing far more rapidly.

Meanwhile a pool of credit one sixth as large as the deposits of all types of banks had accumulated from the reserves of life insurance companies. Life insurance had been unimportant before the Civil War. Many moralists thought it wrong to "gamble" on death. But high-pressure salesmanship stimulated by large commissions and schemes, such as the tontine by which the surviving policyholders of a group received at a fixed date all the money from lapsed policies and accumulated dividends, spread the idea of life insurance. Salesmen made Charlotte Barbier, who had received 74,000 livres on an original subscription of 300 from the first French tontine, as famous as Barbara Fritchie. There were, however, serious students of insurance, such as Elizur Wright, working for state regulations to protect the policyholder and to eliminate gambling.

By 1890 the worst abuses of salesmen and of company relations with policyholders had been corrected, but the investment of insurance reserves for the benefit of the financial interests of certain directors was still to be dealt with. In spite of its checkered early history, a business had been established that was by the mid-twentieth century to have investment reserves about half as large as the deposits of all banks.

Business in 1890. Although the most important changes in the period from 1850 to 1890 involved big companies, the latter were far from typical of American business. Firms of all types were increasing twice as fast as the population. There were about 750,000 business firms in 1880 and more than 1,100,000 by 1890. Compared to this army of entrepreneurs in retailing, wholesaling, service, transportation, finance, and manufacturing, the officers of the few big companies were a corporal's guard. Andrew Carnegie, for example, dominated certain parts of the steel business, but neither he nor any other man controlled the increasing opportunities in hundreds of different types of enterprise scattered from coast to coast. The typical American businessman in every major field of activity except public utilities and railroads operated a small shop with no more than a handful of employees.

In general, business was unregulated by either state or national government. Some old industrial states like Massachusetts restricted the labor of women and children and supervised banking and public utilities, but the federal government had used its powers over interstate commerce only in the case of railroads. Also, the legal meaning of the Interstate Commerce Act of 1887 was far from clear. Antitrust regulation, largely in the interest of small business was in the offing. To the most fearful or perceptive, the shadow of the welfare state was discernible, but it was still a shadow.

— 7 —

BIG BUSINESS AND FINANCE
1890-1929

On January 8, 1889, the august, beetled-browed J. Pierpont Morgan invited a number of the principal railroad presidents to meet in the library of his home on Madison Avenue, New York. There he gave them a lecture on cutthroat competition. He indicated, according to President Roberts of the Pennsylvania, "that we, the railroad people, are a set of anarchists, and this is an attempt to substitute law and order for anarchy and might." The power of Morgan to influence the situation was based on the fact that expanding railroads needed to issue and refund securities, and that he spoke for other leading investment houses. The conference symbolized the growing power of the small group of private banking houses such as Drexel, Morgan; August Belmont; Kidder, Peabody; Kuhn, Loeb; and Lee, Higginson, which were capable of contracting to sell security issues in tens or even hundreds of millions.

As a railroad conference suggests, this influence of security sellers over big business had grown with the rise of railroads and other public utilities. Every big railroad had to raise large amounts of capital by selling stocks and bonds to the general investing public. Telephone, telegraph, power and light companies had to do likewise. A few of the early industrial companies also sold stock to the public. Thus big finance grew hand in hand with big corporations, and both necessitated new social and business adjustments.

Investment Banking. Investment banking was essentially a marketing operation involving wholesaling, retailing, and brokerage. The partners of a security selling house had to calculate the price at which retailers or big investors, like insurance companies, would take the stocks and bonds. Before World War I the domestic market was limited and uncertain, subject to depressed periods when no new security would sell at a reasonable price. Consequently, to be strong a seller of securities needed reliable foreign connections. The half dozen partnerships that handled the biggest American security flotations owed their pre-eminence to such connections. J. Pierpont Morgan rose to great influence through Drexel, Morgan, a New York-Philadelphia alliance at home, J. S. Morgan and Company, his father's house in London, and Morgan, Harjes in Paris. The Barings and Rothschilds of England, and the great continental bankers worked regularly with a few American firms. Kuhn, Loeb and Company of New York was the favored agency for German investment in the United States. For this reason the group that dominated security wholesaling were often called international bankers. (*See Reading No. 9.*)

Because of the risks involved in buying large security issues, even the biggest investment houses formed marketing syndicates. Each member of the syndicate would take a certain part of the issue and pass it on, in turn, to their particular customers, much as insurance companies divided big policies with their competitors. The usual customers of the syndicate members would be foreign banking houses, domestic banks and trust companies, stockbrokers, insurance companies, and individual investors.

Long-run success in the business depended on reliable marketing connections, correct estimates of the immediate market value of securities, and of the prospects of the issuing companies. These considerations necessarily interested the investment bankers in the continuing operations of their clients' business. If Morgan put his name, as syndicate leader, behind an issue he wanted to be sure that the company would be well managed. To accomplish this he, and other American bankers, asked for representation on the board of directors. By 1910, Morgan partners had seventy-two directorships on the boards of

big companies. A further corollary of banker responsibility was continuous relations with the client. The latter
was not supposed to shop around for beter terms for
subsequent security issues. By contriving to oust corporation presidents who disregarded it, Morgan was a leader
in enforcing this principle.

Correct estimate of the market value of new securities
depended upon intimate knowledge of the buyers' psychology and preferably certain controls over their purchasing. This latter could be achieved by influencing the
investment policy of banks and trust and insurance
companies. In these arrangements, Morgan also led the
way. His firm, called J. P. Morgan and Company after
1894, formed close alliances with the two most important
commercial banks, set up two subsidiary trust companies,
and bought large or controlling blocks of the stock in
three leading life insurance companies. Thus by being,
in effect, on both sides of the bargain, Morgan and other
leading investment bankers could normally estimate their
market with some precision. The uncontrollable elements
were the large individual investors and the hundreds of
smaller banks or brokerage houses that valued their connections with the syndicate, but might find securities
unsalable in a sudden swing to bad times. Following the
panic of 1907, for example, the leading investment houses
had to carry many millions of dollars worth of "undi-
gested" new securities to avoid selling them at a large
loss.

Since the investment houses paid the issuing clients
by setting up deposits to their credit, and ran accounts
for large buyers, while the commercial banks sold securities to their depositors, there came to be no sharp distinction between the two types of business. In general,
the investment bankers refused ordinary checking accounts, and put their major emphasis on security marketing, while the commercial banks solicited deposit and
commercial credit accounts, and treated security selling
as a sideline.

The "Money Trust." The group of bankers closely
associated with J. Pierpont Morgan, such as James Stillman, president of the National City Bank, and George F.
Baker, president of the First National Bank of New

York, became so active in consolidating business companies and managing the New York money market that they were investigated in 1911 and 1912 by a Committee of the House of Representatives and condemned as controllers of a "Money Trust."

The bankers could argue that such power as they had was necessitated by the financial situation. James Stillman of National City Bank, for example, presiding over a gold reserve comparable to that of the United States Treasury, and deposits from more than two hundred back-country banks, was partially taking the place of the president of a central bank in the otherwise leaderless anarchy of American banking. In the absence of some government sponsored central system, such private substitutes were bound to develop. But the private system had one great weakness. In times of trouble, National City Bank and the other powerful financial houses had to think of first protecting themselves. They would fulfill their obligations to their own depositors, but could not be expected to make risky loans to help other banks. The policies, therefore, of the biggest New York banks tended to add to, rather than counteract, the pressures of the business cycle.

Undoubtedly, this small group of bankers strongly influenced the investing policies of the major railroads, public utilities, and a good part of heavy industry. In general, the influence was used to merge competitors and to foster conservative financial policies and stable security markets, but occasionally the bankers made wrong guesses. Technical men in companies influenced by the Money Trust saw banker control as a dead hand on innovation and progress. On the other hand, the New York, New Haven and Hartford, and the Chicago, Milwaukee and St. Paul railroads were unwisely expanded under banker guidance to a point where they could no longer make a profit. Certainly, the bankers shared an overconfidence in railroad securities, and a distrust of some new areas of investment, such as the automotive industry.

In assessing the general business affects of concentrated control over large security issues, it must be remembered that only a very small percentage of American firms had any interest in this market. Light industry, wholesaling, retailing, and service, the main areas of business were scarcely affected by the policies of Wall Street bankers. Of 265,000 manufacturing establishments in 1910, scarcely two hundred were big enough to be of importance to investment bankers.

Meanwhile, lesser banking interests had begun the first American venture in foreign banking. In the early years of the century the International Banking Corporation set up small branches in the Far East and the Caribbean area, some of the latter being opened at the request of the State Department. These branches limited themselves to financing trade and providing exchange. In the face of British and other foreign competition, trade financing remained small and would scarcely have supported most of the branches, but buying and selling exchange made high profits for experienced managers. Following a law of 1918 that allowed national banks to own foreign branches, the National City Bank bought the International Banking Corporation. Subsequently, the Chase Bank of New York also established overseas offices.

The Federal Reserve System. In the spring of 1913, while J. Pierpont Morgan was dying in Italy, Congress began consideration of a new banking law designed to institutionalize the functions that he and Baker and Stillman had performed personally. The Federal Reserve Act of 1914, however, did not greatly alter the ordinary business of banking. Those banks that joined the system could now raise cash by rediscounting high-grade commercial paper at their regional Federal Reserve Bank. The majority of smaller banks that did not join could raise cash by rediscounting their paper with a member bank. The major difference was that in times of trouble the member banks had legal access to money, and hence they could lend with greater safety. (*See Reading No. 9.*)

Undoubtedly, the influence of the "Money Trust" was lessened by the Reserve system, but the elder Morgan's death and the effects of massive government financing in World War I weakened the old leadership still more. In the period before American entry into the war, the prestige and influence of J. P. Morgan and Company as the leader of Allied financing was higher than ever be-

fore. But in 1917 the United States Government lifted
the burdens of war finance from the bankers and flooded
the market with Liberty Bonds. By 1919 Liberty and
Victory bonds had created a reserve of readily convertible
savings in the hands of individuals and corporations that
started the easy money market of the 1920's. General
prosperity and easy credit made it possible for syndicates
of small banking and brokerage firms to float large
security issues. The approval of the old houses was no
longer needed in order to raise fifty millions in new
capital.

The Threat of Monopoly.   Some railroads and public utilities had always been big, but manufacturing companies with a hundred million dollars or more in capital
did not appear until the 1880's and 1890's. In a few industries the scale of operations necessary to use machinery most efficiently put a premium on bigness, but more
often the incentive to expansion and mergers was better
control or monopoly of the market. The rate of formation and growth of big companies in the prosperous years
from 1897 to 1904 was so high that many Americans
feared that all business activity was about to fall into
the hands of monopolists.

At this point President Theodore Roosevelt ordered
his Attorney General to enforce the Sherman Anti-Trust
Law of 1890 against the monopolists. (*See Reading No.
11.*) In the ensuing twenty years of intermittent legal
warfare between the Roosevelt, Taft, and Wilson admin-
istrations and big business, a somewhat unstable compromise was reached. In 1911, the United States Supreme
Court ruled that it would have to use its judgment in
deciding whether a monopoly was harmfully restraining
trade, and in 1920 the Court decided that size alone was
an insufficient reason for breaking up a company. On
the other hand, the Court was rigorous in enforcing the
Anti-trust Law against associations of smaller companies
that tried to fix prices and set production quotas.

As a result there emerged in transportation, public
utilities, and the heavy and durable goods industries an
American system of monopolistic competition. From
two or three to a dozen or more companies might
dominate the particular market and sell at nearly uniform

prices, but as long as no one of them tried to swallow
up the others or to acquire stock with a view to lessening
competition, they were regarded as within the law. In
spite of growth and changes in technology, the overall
relations remained surprisingly constant. The percentage
of the labor force engaged in manufacturing, in time of
peace, varied only slightly. Big companies did not greatly
change their position in relation to small and medium-
sized firms.

Management and Control. As the twentieth century progressed, fewer and fewer big companies remained
under individual or family control. The breaking up of
estates by death, selling stock to diversify family investment, and efforts by companies to increase the number
of stockholders spread ownership to thousands of individuals. By 1929 a management that held a substantial
interest in the company, as at Ford or duPont, was rare.
Generally, presidents and other top officers were career
executives promoted on the basis of demonstrated ability.

Boards of directors were less influenced by large stockholders than by the representatives of financial interests,
or by men also holding directorships in other firms that
could be valuable allies, or by representatives of the
company's own management. Wide distribution of stock
meant that in most big companies no group of stockholders could exercise a controlling influence. The tend-
encies inherent in the situation from the start (see
Chapter 4) now became the rule. The board, theo-
retically, elected by the stockholders as their representatives, came in many cases to be nominated by the very
officers who they were supposed to supervise, and the
management slate was regularly elected without opposition. Boards of directors and top managers could only
be challenged by large, outside financial interests capable
of buying or marshaling the votes of millions of shares
of stocks.

As management gained in power, it became more of
a profession. Around the turn of the century, an engineer,
Frederick W. Taylor, began to argue for greater subdivision of both labor and administration, so that each man
could specialize on a single operation, or a particular
kind of know-how. (*See Reading No. 8.*) He worked out

schemes for "functional" management that were too elaborate and rigorous for most companies, but which influenced business thinking. The rise of college education in accounting, industrial engineering, management, and marketing was another force for greater specialization in administration. The greater size of companies worked in the same direction. If new departments had to be set up in order to handle the increasing volume of business, it was wise to think of possible readjustments of functions in order to increase efficiency.

The overall result of these forces was to circumscribe the authority of "line" officials such as foremen, shop superintendents, and production managers and to vest authority in "staff" departments for special purposes. The foreman, for example, had become a small czar in the nineteenth-century shop, hiring, firing, promoting, and planning work. By 1920 in advanced companies he had lost these functions to personnel, training, engineering, and planning departments. Instead of being a manager he had become a limited type of supervisor.

Personnel departments, introduced rapidly during the labor shortages of World War I, focused attention on general problems of morale. Employing new psychological theories, personnel experts pictured the company as a working community to which members should be bound by loyalty and sentiment. This seemed particularly desirable in companies so large that personal contact was infrequent between lower and top management. Employee clubs, teams, and magazines were useful devices for pulling the organization together. The first issue of *The Lamp*, in 1918, said: "Its purpose is to introduce the employees of Standard Oil Company (New Jersey) to each other and to cultivate acquaintanceship into a spirit of fellowship and cordial cooperation."

While for general morale it was good to knit the company together, for certain operations it seemed best to decentralize. Setting up semi-autonomous divisions had been the aim of some advanced business thinkers from the 1870's on, but the full and careful application of such plans came in most companies after World War I. (*See Reading No. 10.*) As Donaldson Brown of General Motors told the American Management Association in

1927: The "problem is to combine the economical advantages of modern business, with as little sacrifice as possible of that intimate control and development of managerial ability that is the character of a well managed small business."

Let the local manager make the kind of day-to-day operating decisions that he would make if it were his own business, but let him rely for policy on the vast intellectual apparatus of the big corporation. The committee was an essential technique in applying such a policy. Here members of top management, and of appropriate staff departments, would sit with the local operating head to discuss his problems. By being on many standing committees for different purposes, executives came to know each other and a wider range of company problems than went through their own offices.

During the twenties, duPont and General Motors worked out complex structures to balance and coordinate central and local authority. In general, the aim was to free top executives from routine problems. As the result of a study by a Co-Ordination Committee in 1925, for example, Standard Oil of New Jersey delegated operating and development problems to subsidiaries and left the officers and directors of the old parent company with no immediate responsibilities. Thus, the highest officers became a planning board or committee for long-range policy.

Marketing. Big companies controlling a substantial share of the national market also developed new methods of selling. Before the 1890's, factories had depended upon traveling salesmen and local wholesalers and jobbers to sell their wares. Only patent medicine makers like Lydia Pinkham and a few producers of branded goods for the consumer like Pears Soap or Royal Baking Powder carried on nation-wide advertising. In the decade of the nineties the situation changed rapidly. Manufacturers were discovering the value of publicized brands and packages. Companies making cereals, crackers, canned goods, beer, and dozens of similar products began trying to reach all housewives. Even makers of equipment for other businessmen began to advertise. There were new media to carry the messages. The total

circulation of newspapers and magazines in 1890 had
been about thirty million, by 1900 it was four times as
large. The quality had also changed. Cheap slick paper
magazines like *The Saturday Evening Post, Ladies' Home
Journal, Munsey's,* and *McClure's* were printed in attractive formats with many illustrations and stories
carried back which led the reader to the advertising.

The automobile and bicycle gave new importance to
signs and billboards, while cards in trolleys, elevateds,
and subways provided a new media. By 1900 a bigger
part of the national income was being spent on advertising than in the years after World War II, and by 1910
the amount had risen to a high plateau of over 4 per
cent of all income, which, except for the war years, was
maintained until 1929.

Advertising agencies hired artists to design arresting
copy, retained consulting psychologists to plan emotional
appeal, and gave increasing attention to the type of
public reached by various media. An advertising executive said in 1905: "Our great business is to show the
manufacturer that he ought to own his own trade by
making the demand direct from the consumer." Advertising managers in manufacturing firms became important
executives, whereas a few years before they had been
regarded as routine employees.

The effect was not only to increase consumer expenditure particularly on durable goods, but also to create
new ties between factory and retailer. Goods might now
bypass wholesalers, and the factory might assist the retailer in local display and advertising. The rise of the
department store, mail-order house, and chain store
marked further steps in the elimination of middlemen.

Macy's and Wanamaker's department stores in New
York and Philadelphia went back to the Civil War, but
the rapid spread of this type of retailing came after 1890.
Not only did the new stores add to the convenience and
lower the cost of shopping, but they necessarily did away
with bargaining and introduced the principle of a single
price. In many of the items sold, control of production
rested with the store that placed special orders with
manufacturers.

By the turn of the century the mail-order catalogue

was one of the most important agencies of rural marketing. Sears, Roebuck, for example, was transferring goods
from its especially commissioned suppliers to the customer
with a minimum of distributing cost. Furthermore, for
pianos or other costly durables the mail-order house
would arrange installment payments.

The automobile companies that reached their customers
directly through retail dealers pushed installment buying
to new heights in the 1920's. General Motors set up its
own credit agency to finance both new and used-car purchases. As the big motor makers spread into the manufacture of refrigerators, vacuum cleaners, and radios in
competition with the electrical equipment makers, installment selling spread to almost all types of durable consumer goods. But housing remained bound by the
traditional banking arrangements of large down payments
and long-term fixed mortgages.

Chains, such as Atlantic and Pacific Tea Company,
Kroger food stores or Woolworth's five and ten, growing
rapidly after 1900, appeared to threaten the ultimate ex-
tinction not only of the wholesaler but of the independent
retailer as well. According to a leading authority, "the
retail distribution of staple groceries received for the
first time the sustained attention and direction of administrators of a high order of business ability." Well-managed chain operations in food may have cut the cost of
distribution by a third. Chain-store sales rose from 4 per
cent of all retail sales in 1919 to 22 per cent in 1929.
Ultimately, independently owned stores secured comparable advantages by forming "voluntary" chains of wholesalers and retailers, and the expansion of corporate chains
was checked, but the strength of this later movement was
not evident in the 1920's.

Public Relations. World War I had several lasting
affects upon American business. In estimating or ap-
portioning supplies in many lines, government administrators found it convenient to work through trade
associations. This gave added strength and prestige to
existing associations and led to forming hundreds of new
ones. The war also gave a number of war contractors
high profits, which were subsequently invested in new
types of enterprise, such as airplanes, chemicals, and elec-

trical equipment. But even more important was the growth of modern public relations. (*See Reading No. 12.*)

The origins of public relations, the building of a favorable public image of a company, or industry, go far back. Congressional lobbyists, such as John L. Hayes of the wool manufacturers, or James Swanck of the iron and steel association, who represented their organizations during the post-Civil War decades, were also public relations men. They both wrote and inspired articles and gave out convincingly factual news releases. Their statistics were accurate enough to serve as a basis for both Congressional and scholarly argument. Railroad executives sponsored books and articles that would present the industry to the public in a more favorable light. In the 1890's, George Harvey did public relations work for urban traction interests. But these were isolated instances and these pioneers never started public relations agencies.

George Creel's Committee on Public Information that supplied the American propaganda for World War I was the great training school for public relations men. Armed with new British and French ideas and the psychology of Sigmund Freud, they developed theories about subconscious motivation, of how to form public opinion by indirect pressures, which earlier men had only partially realized from experience.

As soon as the war was over, Edward Bernays, Ivy Lee, and others associated with the work of the Creel committee opened offices for public relations counseling. Advertising agencies pushed this new dimension with their customers. A few big companies added public relations departments. The techniques used in the 1920's reflected the journalistic or advertising background of the early operators. Favorable news releases, often forced on editors under threat of loss of advertising, articles planted in magazines, moving pictures, and paid advertisements were the stock in trade. They all belonged to the "puff" or nonsubstantial type of public relations. Few men of the period tried to get business to change its practices to conform better with public desires, or to allocate business resources for public welfare.

Another type of public relations, not usually labeled as such, was increase in the number of stockholders. Com-

panies like A. T. & T. put on continuous campaigns to
spread ownership among more of the public. Five hundred thousand stockholders were half a million friends of
the company ready to resist regulation or the remote
possibility of government control. Such ideas led to split-
ting stocks into more shares with a lower price and to
efforts to please and compliment stockholders. Annual
reports were made attractive and easy to read. Letters
from the president were addressed to the stockholders
from time to time, and they were polled for their pref-
erences regarding products.

Prelude to Disaster. Other new developments of
the 1920's in the area of big business were to have less
happy results. The easy money market partly created by
the exchange of billions in government Liberty and Victory bonds for securities with more promise of income
and gain led to new financial practices. Instead of borrowing from banks, expanding companies found it easier to
issue stock, and banks come to make more and more of
their loans with stocks and bonds rather than goods, in-
voices, or bills of lading as security. It became easy to sell
a five or ten million dollar mortgage on a hotel, office
building, or real estate development by dividing it into
thousand-dollar shares and selling them to small investors.
For the little man who wanted to diversify his holdings,
investment trusts promised that their stock would give
him the benefit of their management's judgment in buying and selling securities.

To gain control of large numbers of operating concerns
with a limited amount of capital, financiers like the Van
Schweringen Brothers of Cleveland, or Samuel Insull of
Chicago, set up complex pyramids of holding companies,
in which the investing public provided the necessary capital. Such combinations, particularly in public utilities,
were thought to promise almost unlimited future earnings,
and their stocks became market favorites.

However, while the financial structure became more top-
heavy, the ordinary activities of business moved smoothly.
In spite of hard times in such lines as textiles, farming, or
country banking, 1928 and the first three quarters of 1929
were a time of general satisfaction and complacence.
Partly because of the public relations men, and partly

because of prosperity, American business leaders enjoyed a better reputation than ever before. Instead of fearing monopoly, most people took pride in big American companies. If one could save only a little money and put it in common stocks, the continual growth of big companies would bring personal security. To most urban businessmen the situation in 1929 seemed promising: wages and prices were steady, inventories were well adjusted to demand, new building was continuing. The only unusual features were the continuing rise in stock prices and interest rates and the relentless pressure of salesmen with foreign securities. Even the few prophets of doom, such as business forecaster Roger Babson, were unprepared for the cataclysm of the 1930's.

— 8 —

BUSINESS IN A NEW SETTING

From the days of Adam Smith to those of Herbert Hoover, businessmen and all but a few American politicians had believed that the economy should regulate itself. Government aid had been offered in the nineteenth century, and there had always been some regulation, but such acts were regarded as exceptions to, or minor modifications of, the normal rule of economic law. After 1932, government, particularly the previously remote federal government, became so involved in the management of the economy that self-regulation or the unhampered operation of economic "laws" became remote ideals, having little to do with reality.

The Partnership with Government.   The resulting partnership of big business and big government went through two distinct phases. The first, from 1932 to 1940,

was one in which business sought government help and
was then appalled by the forces that had been set in motion. The era was initiated in 1932 by loans to, or investment in the preferred stocks, of banks, railroads, and
other hard-pressed companies by the Reconstruction
Finance Corporation. The National Industrial Recovery
Act of a year later was also designed in accordance with
general business desires, but from there on the Roosevelt
Administration went too far and too fast for a happy
partnership. By 1934 most businessmen felt that the
government was hostile to them, and this feeling prevailed
until World War II.

Furthermore, the reputation of big business had been
so shattered by the economic collapse from 1930 to 1932,
and by resulting scandals in high and low finance, that
business leaders felt powerless to defend themselves
against unwanted legislation. In the 1920's the words of a
Morgan partner were often more important than those of
the President of the United States; by 1933 the friendly
voice of FDR carried more influence than all the leading
businessmen combined.

Three laws in particular seemed nearly intolerable to
most businessmen. The Securities Act of 1933, modeled
on earlier European statutes, placed restriction and lia-
bilities on the issuers of stocks and bonds. Far more information than had been voluntarily included in prospec-
tuses now had to be supplied to the buyer. The income
tax law of 1935, called the "soak the rich" act, raised sur-
taxes to a point where they virtually prevented large net
income. But most objectionable of all was the National
Labor Relations Act of this same year, known as the
Wagner Act. (See Reading No. 11.)

American management, believing firmly in the open
shop, had been able to restrict organized labor to the
skilled crafts, a diminishing area, and to company sponsored unions. The National Recovery Act, by imposing
an obligation on management to bargain collectively, had
somewhat increased the size of the American Federation
of Labor, but had added still more to the ranks of company unions. In contrast, the Wagner Act prohibited employers from taking any part in the relations between
their employees and unions. Management could not issue

letters or notices that would influence workers in choosing their bargaining agent, or exclude organizers from the plant. A union could call for an election whenever they thought best, and management had to deal with the group that won a majority of the employee votes. In cases of disagreement final appeal was to be made to the National Labor Relations Board, which employers regarded as pro-labor.

Seizing their opportunity, a group of young organizers like Walter Reuther swept the employees of rubber, autos, and steel into the ranks of the new Congress of Industrial Organizations. For big company managements that before 1933 had never had seriously to consider industry-wide unionism, the world was in truth turned upside down.

To make matters worse, the New Deal measures failed to bring any lasting prosperity. In most business existing capacity seemed adequte for demand, and there was no incentive to invest for expansion. In addition, it was widely believed that the upswing from 1933 to 1937 depended upon government spending. When a move toward balancing the budget was followed by severe recession the case seemed proved.

Preparation for war in 1940 brought a new turning point in the relations of government and business. Now the government started spending for the products of private industry instead of for relief or made work. While the level of expenditure far exceeded that of the depression and added astronomically to the national debt, it stimulated private investment and diminished unemployment. There were frictions, of course, particularly when Roosevelt moved to step up defense spending at the expense of consumer goods in the summer and fall of 1941, but economically the situation became increasingly satisfactory. As Paul Litchfield of Goodyear said: "I think everyone who had to do with our aircraft work came out of the war with a deep feeling of satisfaction over it."

At the end of the war, businessmen found themselves in a new world. Wages were higher than had ever been dreamed of, but consumer demand was beyond filling. It seemed clear that this situation was the result of massive government spending. When demand started to slacken in 1949, the mere promise of an increase in spending, voted by a conservative Congress, was enough to start things up again. Then wars, Korean and cold, brought nearly full employment, shortages, and inflation until 1957.

In this last period the level of government military expenditure, running about 20 per cent of the national income, was a powerful force for continued stability. Since money did not have to be spent in the fiscal year for which it was appropriated, contracts could be let or held back with a view to adjusting supply and demand. New plant investment and relocation were stimulated by quick write-off of the cost against taxes. Such older federal government expenditures as those for education, roads, or veterans seemed small by comparison.

Although government continued to harass big business by enforcement of the antitrust laws, more actions being brought in the forties than ever before, the corporate and personal income tax laws encouraged mergers. Companies suffering losses could carry them over to succeeding years as a deduction from taxable profits. This made a firm with so-called tax losses valuable to a company that was making big profits, and management practices had become so uniform and well understood that big companies did not hesitate to buy firms in other lines of business.

Furthermore, since capital gains were taxed at a low fixed rate and personal income taxes mounted progressively to very high rates, the best way to get money out of a business was to sell it. Thus, there was a pressure for the small businessman to sell out to a larger firm as soon as he had achieved marked success, and to try to build another enterprise. While this made for bigger business units, it kept smart entrepreneurs on the move.

During this generation of prosperity, businessmen came to live with and even to appreciate some of the New Deal legislation. Social security and unemployment insurance were accepted as good in principle, and many companies provided additions to government pension payments. Government commissions became mellower with age and the addition of members from industry. Collective bargaining, as modified by the more conservative Taft-Hartley law of 1947, was in line with new ideas regarding the productive value of high employee morale. The Full Employment

Act of 1946 which set up the President's Committee of Economic Advisors, and affirmed the government's duty to stabilize the economy, was accepted with little comment on the clearly implied principle of government planning. The partnership appeared to be going smoothly.

The Vital Statistics of Business. As big businesses grew bigger, small businesses multiplied. Up to 1950 firms of every size increased in numbers faster than the population. In 1900 there were a million and a quarter firms listed by Dun & Bradstreet in a country with 75 million people; in 1950 considerably more than twice that many firms were listed for only twice as many people. After 1950 the rate of population increase began to outstrip that of new business units, but the shift was too moderate to prove a new trend.

Among individual companies, big ones, no matter what level of assets be taken as big, grew the most. A sample of the largest companies collected in 1928 showed 13 per cent with sales exceeding fifty million dollars a year; a nearly identical sample in 1952 had 13 per cent with more than five hundred million dollars a year. Beneath these thousand or so giant companies, American business included more than thirty thousand "medium" sized firms that had sales of over five hundred thousand dollars a year in 1947 and below this moderate level were nearly four million smaller firms.

Continued growth in every size of enterprise mirrored the fact that more of the efforts of the society were being devoted to business, particularly to trade and commercial service, and relatively less to agriculture and household work. As industrialism progressed it ramified in variety. Every year brought new products, perhaps made at the start by a single worker. New products meant new types of trade and repairs, and new personal services. Big firms added departments, such as market research, unthought of by earlier generations and thus multiplied the types of careers available in the bureaucratic areas of business. As industry spread south and west, business opportunities increased in the farming areas. So each generation of Americans from 1790 on had a greater variety of careers to choose from. In addition, research in the 1950's indicated that the boy with nothing in back of him save education and ability had an increasing chance of rising toward the top as business grew bigger and less dominated by family influence.

The company pattern was one of continuous births, deaths, and mergers. In a normal year around mid-century, 400,000 to 500,000 new firms would be formed, and nearly that many would disappear for one reason or another, of which a thousand or two would be merged to form larger units. New lines tended to start with many small operators. As time went on, mergers would take place and already big companies would enter the field. After thirty years the hundred-odd automobile manufacturers were reduced to half a dozen. But meanwhile, dozens of new lines would be in the early stage of small firms. History seemed to indicate that, with free enterprise, only a failure of the economy to progress technologically could eliminate small business.

but this

Marketing. Production problems became relatively minor in established American industries. In big business particularly, patent licensing and pools, and the impossibility of keeping trade secrets in a vast organization, made for uniformity in processes and products. Fear of the destructive effects of price warfare on heavily capitalized industry led firms to follow certain price leaders or the published prices of their competitors. The real pressure for innovation, for new ideas, was in methods of marketing. In a highly competitive industry like brewing, a new advertising slogan might sell a million barrels. New styling in a portable radio could sweep away sales from competitors.

As Americans were able to buy more and more durable goods, such as refrigerators, radios, or automobiles, or nonessential luxuries of other kinds, sales managers realized that every producer was competing for the same dollars even though their products might be different. The small-income family that bought a radio had to put off buying a new vacuum cleaner; similarly, perfume competed with hats or handbags. This wide range of choice in purchasing made for a less calculable kind of competition. The products of an entire industry might sell well or poorly in any given year.

To lessen such hazards, producers and advertising

agencies undertook or sponsored market research. Consumers were polled to determine their probable future desires. Shopping and reading habits, and family budgets were studied. Intelligent buying was found to correlate with education and, as general levels of income and education advanced, competition promised to be keener and customer requirements more important.

Almost universal use of automobiles, outside the center of big cities, and the pressures of the great depression combined to increase the size of retail units. Corporate chains closed down many stores and added to the size of those remaining. Chain novelty stores, such as Grant, Woolworth, or Kresge, expanded their lines and price range so that they began to resemble department stores, while old style department stores were organized in chains.

The most spectacular innovation of the early 1930's was the self-service supermarket. Soon the big food chains started using supermarkets, and local chains of three or four markets appeared. There was considerable saving to the customer in buying at a supermarket which could reduce the amount paid for labor per unit of sales and buy in large quantities. But the small food retailer still survived, particularly in the congested areas of big cities. He was near the customer's home, established personal relations, had few or no paid employees, granted credit, and made deliveries. For these conveniences many customers were willing to pay 10 or 20 per cent more.

Small retailers, particularly in drugs, cosmetics, and durable goods, feared price cutting by larger dealers or chains. In the early 1930's associated retailers won "fair trade" laws in 44 states which permitted the negotiation of binding resale contracts between producers and distributors. In 1937, the Miller-Tydings Bill amended the Sherman Anti-Trust Act to permit such contracts in interstate commerce. Only about 15 per cent of retail trade was affected by price agreements, but even in these cases illegal discounts were frequent, and court decisions weakened the force of the laws. Meanwhile, there was a continuing effort by big producers to eliminate price competition at the factory level and in national advertising while permitting or even encouraging price cutting by dealers.

The explosive exodus to the suburbs and country areas around big cities that came with the building boom after World War II increased the tendency to shop by automobile at large markets rather than small neighborhood stores. Central city department stores found that it paid to establish suburban branches, and surround them with shopping centers including all the kinds of stores that the housewife normally visited. There was also a trend toward arterial highway locations that could attract through as well as local trade. The old main street of a town might become unimportant as a shopping area.

Managerial Enterprise. Although small business-men still constituted at least 90 per cent of the six million "proprietors and managers" listed in the Census of 1950, the group that managed the thousand largest corporations had far more than their numerical share of influence. These top executives of large companies were well-educated professionals assumed to possess outstanding managerial ability. Having specialists in their service, they could present the newest ideas. The large resources under their control gave them economic power and social prestige. Although the group was small, it was steadily increasing in size as more medium-sized companies grew and expanded their managements.

The big company managers of the mid-twentieth century had mainly risen through the ranks: only a quarter of them had been independent businessmen. Their rise had depended not only on ability to make decisions and administer people, but also on their being able to make friends and create a smooth running organization. Frank Abrams, president of Standard Oil Company of New Jersey, stated the logical result of thinking in terms of the welfare of the organization. "Modern management," he said, "might well measure its success or failure as a profession in large part by the satisfactions it is able to produce for its employees."

Emphasis on the company as an organization to provide satisfying careers for its employees suggests profound changes in the motives behind business leadership. Granted that in a competitive system that profits, security, and satisfaction for the individual are all closely related, differences in emphasis produce differences in behavior.

(*See Reading No. 10.*) In an economy regulated by government, longrun security, for example, might be better served by moderate rather than maximum profit. "There is not only no incentive," said W. A. Gifford of A. T. & T. in 1927, "but it would be contrary to sound policy for the management to earn speculative or large profits." There was also a tendency to think of profits as belonging first of all to "the company" rather than to the stockholders.

More authority, adventure, and satisfaction for the upper-middle level executive was one of the forces behind decentralization through divisions or subsidiaries. A man at the head of an autonomous division, that bought its own materials, made its own products, and then marketed them, might not even be an officer in the big company, but he had most of the excitements and responsibilities of an independent businessman. Of 124 representative large corporations polled in 1955, 75 per cent had some operations under division managements. (*See Reading No. 10.*) Whether a company spread authority by divisions or corporate subsidiaries was usually a matter of tax policy, or an adjustment to state or national laws. In either case the principle was to fight bureaucratic inertia and discontent by presenting the manager with risk and power.

A new emphasis emerged in dealing with labor. Managers at the bargaining table were meeting fellow employees, members of the organization with whom they had to work. While union representatives, as such, were to be resisted, good wages and salaries benefited all members of the company. Furthermore, if prices were administered by the firms that set the wage scales, increases could be passed on to the consumer. Since the big company, therefore, could adjust rather easily to moderate inflationary trends, its managerial enterprise was less adamant against increases in cost than the small businessman who feared for his competitive position.

Since executives expected pensions from the company upon retirement, they looked far ahead, and long-range policy was in the hands of management. In some big companies everyone on the board of directors was a salaried manager and the stockholders, as such, were not represented. The managerial emphasis on longevity and security showed in many ways. Large reserves against future contingencies took precedence over dividends. Investment in research that would develop new products or improve old ones became a major device for insuring the company's market position. Investment was made in new lines to gain security by diversification of products and services. Thus some big companies were competing in dozens of fields, in some of which their share of the market might be fairly small. In spite of competition, however, most big companies demonstrated a strong ability to survive.

Economic Democracy. Troubled on occasion by a need to find a basis in the American political tradition for their broad practical authority, managers developed the concept of consumer democracy. Through buying its products, consumers cast votes in favor of the management of the company. If the public ceased buying, the company would fail and its management be changed. Therefore, management, like government, depended on popular support. While patents, monopolies, and other limitations on consumer choice weakened this argument, there was unquestionably a trend in management toward more regard for democratic principles both within and outside the company.

Part of the force behind this trend was a recognition that democracy was good for production. Professor Elton Mayo's book, *The Human Problems of an Industrial Civilization,* written in 1933, provided convincing evidence that workers with relatively good pay wanted respect for their dignity and acceptance as members of a community more than higher wages. These findings touched off a good deal of thinking regarding morale in the ranks of both labor and management. The manpower shortages of World War II brought such lessons home to many managers unaffected by theoretical findings, but as late as the 1950's some companies were discovering for the first time that employees produced more when they understood and approved company policies.

The same type of reasoning applied to lower and middle management. Conferences and group decisions in which those concerned could participate brought better responses than arbitrary orders from above. Democratic procedures, or "bottom-up" management as it came to be called, allowed executives to tap the abilities of those who might never enter the circle of the chosen few at the top. To further the idea of autonomy in middle management, some big companies, instead of subjecting managers who had made poor showings to lectures by top executives, found it better simply to send statistics indicative of performance to the managers involved and let them try to work out their own solutions.

More participation in policy procedures throughout the ranks was in harmony with an increasing emphasis on committee work and group decisions at the top. Business operation was seen increasingly in terms of cooperation and teamwork, even to the extent of executives in one firm wearing uniform company sports blazers to conferences.

Many executives were not convinced of the value of "bottom-up" procedures. In 1957, Robert N. McMurry, a management consultant, said: "I have been studying a number of instances of socalled 'democratic-participative management' in large-scale operation and, frankly, I don't think it functions very well." He thought few top executives were truly in sympathy with such procedures and he favored a "benevolent" aristocracy. Perhaps the most forceful argument of observers like Mr. McMurry was that middle management inevitably became staffed by bureaucrats who preferred to "live by the book."

New Public Relations.   The interest of management in planning and long-run trends and the hostile criticisms of the 1930's brought a new regard for public opinion. It was now clear that public relations had to be something more than pious statements of good will or glorification of past achievements. Advertising executive A. H. Batten said in 1937: "Any public relations worthy of the name must . . . meet at every point the test of good citizenship and usefulness to the community." Public relations came to be seen by its advocates as a two-way street down which the ideas and desires of business reached the public, and ideas from the latter went back to business.

An interest in good community relations was far from universal even in big business. Prior to court decisions of the 1950's many managements held that they had no right to spend stockholders' money on community welfare. Some still doubted that better relations with workers and their families could improve productivity. But after World War II more and more executives of the giant companies recognized that, because of their economic power, they themselves were an important part of the public. (*See Reading No. 12.*)

High income and inheritance taxes led scores of companies to set up tax-free foundations that could absorb earnings and hold stocks. The foundations devoted their resources to welfare or research, some of which might, in turn, be useful to the company. By mid-century there were a thousand foundations.

This considerable growth in company activities not immediately connected with profit-making particularly benefited cities that depended for their economic life on one or two branch plants of big companies. Branch managers came to take a leading part in civic affairs and were empowered to make substantial company contributions to local causes. Whether some welfare activities depended largely on continuous prosperity and nearly full employment remained to be seen.

Business at Mid-Century. By mid-century, corporate executives and even small businessmen were harassed by the complexity of the business system. More books, articles, reports, and company memoranda than anyone could read piled up in each office. There were more meetings of committees and associations than one could attend, and more possible schemes that might bring advantage than one could pursue. The number of organizations ready to serve a businessman had become too numerous to be known to anyone but a devotee of the subject. To the older trade and employers' associations were added management, accounting, engineering, and other societies whose aim was to advance business knowledge and interests. Special service organizations, such as the Exchange, Kiwanis, Lions, Rotary, and other clubs, brought them together for lunch or entertainment. To some degree these many formal organizations only compensated for the enforced isolation of specialists, but they unquestionably raised the level of expertness and the volume of communication.

Since 1932 government policy had become a major consideration for all successful businessmen. For big manufacturing or transportation companies there were government contracts to be won that might make the difference between annual profit or loss. Smaller manufacturers fought for subcontracts, and all companies adjusted their expectations on the basis of proposed government spending. Major business decisions usually involved tax considerations. "Carry-over" losses, rates of depreciation, capital gains as against income, all had to be considered, and this required legal experts.

Although the business leader of the 1950's might feel himself much less master of the world with which he had to deal than had Carnegie or Morgan, there were certain compensations. The partnership with government insured more stability in the economy. Government spending, social insurance, and financial controls had helped tame the ferocious American business cycle. Ever higher wages brought continued inflation and gave consumers more choice as to what they would buy, but high average incomes also increased demand.

For the man rising through the ranks of medium- or large-sized business, there was more security than ever before and more possibilities of specialization. To prevent security from superseding risk-taking, departments were established to suggest new ideas and developments. Yet a general opinion among businessmen was that a cautious careerism and high taxes combined to make management less willing to take risks than in earlier days.

Big companies were accounting for an increasingly large percentage of business income; but by adopting cooperative methods of buying and by entering into supply contracts with larger firms, small business was still flourishing in industry and trade. As people became more prosperous, service operations grew, and remained largely in the hands of individual proprietors. Looking at business in terms of men rather than dollars of sales, small operators continued to typify American enterprise.

The American position of world leadership confronted business with a problem never seriously considered by earlier generations: Did business beliefs and practices conform to the democratic traditions that the United

States was trying to strengthen? From the paternal control of apprentices and journeymen by masters to clear
lines of control from the top in early big business, managerial authortiy was accepted by American society as a
law of nature. But, starting in 1933, government regulations rapidly restricted managerial action. In the forties
labor leaders like Walter Reuther began to question the
prerogatives of management. To this outside pressure was
gradually added the belief by certain professional executives that it was best to have broad discussion of new
policies, to give lower management a sense that its
opinions were being regarded.

Such external and internal limitations on managerial
authority were, to be sure, only approaches to democracy,
but in the long history of business on this continent they
could mark an important new trend. If this were the case,
American culture would present fewer contradictions to
foreigners, and businessmen might become stronger representatives of the main traditions of American democracy.

Part II

DOCUMENTS

— Reading No. 1 —

CONDITIONS OF SETTLEMENT[1]

I

The agreement entered into by the Pilgrims in 1620 in order to gain transportation to America illustrates the relationship between settlers and investors in England. The Pilgrims thought the terms "very afflictive to the minds of such as were concerned in the voyage, and hard enough for the poor people, that were to adventure their persons as well as their estates." This feeling that they were being exploited by the absentee owners was held by settlers in other colonies financed by stock companies.

✓   ✓   ✓

1. The Adventurers and Planters do agree that every person that goeth, being sixteen years old and upwards, be rated at ten pounds, and that ten pounds be accounted a single share.

[1] For I, William Bradford, *History of the Plimouth Plantation* (Boston, 1900), pp. 56-58; and Alexander Young, *Chronicles of the Pilgrim Fathers of the Colony of Plymouth from 1602-1625* (Boston, 1841), p. 97. For II, Virginia Company—Instructions to George Yeardley, November 18, 1618, Document in Library of Congress—Miscellaneous Records, 1606-1692, pp. 72-77, as quoted in *Records of the Virginia Company of London,* ed., Susan Kingsbury, Vol. III, p.103. For III, Beauchamp Plantagenet, *A Description of the Province of New Albion,* 1648, in Force, *Tracts and Other Papers* (Washington, 1838), II no. vii, 31-36.

2. That he goeth in person, and furnisheth himself out with ten pounds, either in money or other provisions, be accounted as having twenty pounds in stock, and in the division shall receive a double share.

3. The persons transported, and the Adventurers, shall continue their joint stock and partnership the space of seven years, except some unexpected impediments do cause the whole company to agree otherwise; during which time all profits and benefits that are gotten by trade, traffic, trucking, working, fishing, or any other means, of any other person or persons, shall remain still in the common stock until the division.

4. That at their coming there, they shall choose out such a number of fit persons as may furnish their ships and boats for fishing upon the sea; employing the rest in their several faculties upon the land, as building houses, tilling and planting the ground, and making such commodities as shall be most useful for the Colony.

5. That at the end of the seven years, the capital and the profits, namely, the houses, lands, goods, and chattels, be equally divided among the Adventurers.

6. Whoever cometh to the Colony hereafter, or putteth anything into stock, shall, at the end of the seven years, be allowed proportionally, to the time of his so doing.

7. He that shall carry his wife, or children, or servants, shall be allowed for every person now aged sixteen years and upwards, a single share in the division; or if he provide them with necessaries, a double share; or if they be between ten years old and sixteen, then two of them to be reckoned a person, both in transportation and division.

8. That such children as now go, and are under the age of ten years have no other share in the division than fifty acres of unmanured land.

9. That such persons as die before the seven years be expired, their executors to have their parts or share at the division, proportionately to the time of their life in the Colony.

10. That all such persons as are of the Colony to have meat, drink, apparel, and all provisions, out of the common stock and goods of said Colony.

The Pilgrims' conscientious effort to live up to the contract is shown in a letter from Edward Winslow to a friend in England on December 11, 1621.

✓   ✓   ✓

When it pleaseth God we are settled and fitted for the fishing business and oher trading, I doubt not but by the blessing of God the gain will give content to all. In the mean time, that we have gotten we have sent by this ship; and though it be not much, yet it will witness for us that we have not been idle, considering the smallness of our number all this summer. We hope the merchants will accept of it, and be encouraged to furnish us with things needful for further employment, which will also encourage us to put forth ourselves to the uttermost.

II

As shown in these instructions to the Governor of Virginia in 1618, stockholders saw the economies to be derived from replacing imports by local manufacture.

✓   ✓   ✓

And for the better Encouragement of all sorts of necessary and laudable trades to be set up and exercised within the said four Cities and Burroughs We do hereby ordain that if any artizans or tradesmen shall be desirous rather to follow his particular Art or trade than to be imployed in husbandry or other rural business It shall be lawful for you the said Governor and Council to alot and set out within any of the precincts aforesaid One dwelling house with four Acres of land adjoining and held in fee simple to every said tradesman his heirs and Assigns for ever upon condition that the said tradesman his heirs and Assigns do continue and exercise his trade in the said house paying only a fee rent of four pence by the year to us the said Treasurer and Company and our Successors at the feast of St. Michael the Archangel for ever.

III

The cost of settlement in the mid-seventeenth century and the rewards offered by proprietors to individuals who transport settlers in wholesale lots are illustrated in the promotional prospectus for a proprietary colony in North Carolina in 1648.

✓   ✓   ✓

PROVISIONS FOR EACH MAN, AND
CHARGE FROM LONDON

1. Canvas, or linnen clothes, Shooes, Hats &c. costing here foure pounds for two men to buy Cows, Goats, and Hogs in *Virginia,* which there yeeld six pound, and will buy one Cow and Oxe, two Goats two Sowes, which one each man comes to   2 £ 00

2. Fraight for a Passenger, and his half Tun of provisions and Tooles.   1 £ 10. 0

3. Victuals till his own stock and crop maintain him for seven moneths.   3. £ 10. 0

That is Pease, Oatmeal and Aquavite, 7s. five bushels of Meal, of which to be baked into Biskets, and five bushels of Malt, some must be ground and brewed for the voyage, both 1 l. 10s. a hundred of Beefe, and Pork, 1 l 2s. two bushels of roots, 2 s. salt fish, 2 s. Cask to carry provisions 5 s. five pound of Butter 2 s.

4. One Hogshead of eares of Corn Garden seeds, Hemp, and linseed with husk and some Rice from *Virginia.*   0. 16. 0

5. Armies (*viz*) a Sword, Calliver five foot long, or long Pistoll, Pikehead: six pound of powder, ten pound of shot, halfe an old slight Armour that is, two to one Armour.   0. 19. 0

6. Tools, a Spade, Axe, and Shovell, 5 s. Iron and Steel to make and men more, and two hundred of nails, 5 s.   0. 10. 0

7. Guns and Powder for the Fort, that is

to every fifty foure Murtherers a barell of
powder 4 1. 10 s. that is to each man.   5 s.
   8. A Bed and sheets of Canvas, to be filled
with Juls, each man a Rug.   15. a
                        Sum totall,   10 £ 5. 0

          .   .   .   .   .

   All Adventurers of 500 1. to bring fifty men shall have
5000 acres, and a manor with Royalties, at 5 s. rent,
and whosoever is willing so to transport himself or servant
at 10 1. a man, shall for each man have 100 acres granted
forever. . . . All which [transported servants] after 5
years service, are to have 30 acres of free land, and some
stock, and bee free-holders.

✔ — Reading No. 2 —

MERCHANTS AND CRAFTSMEN²

I

*The Calvinist attitude of frugality, temperance, and
devotion to work is shown in the precepts that Benjamin
Franklin in his middle twenties drew up for his own guidance. The pervasiveness of these attitudes is suggested by
the fact that Franklin himself belonged to no church. Thus
Puritanism or Calvinism as a force in American business*

² For I, *The Autobiography of Benjamin Franklin,* Every-
   man's Library (New York: Dutton, 1908), pp 99-100.
   For II, W. T. Baxter, *The House of Hancock: Business
   in Boston 1724-1775* (Cambridge: Harvard University
   Press, 1945), pp. 185-186. For III, Edward Gray, *William
   Gray of Salem, Merchant* (Boston: Houghton, Mifflin,
   1914), pp. 13-6. For IV, Carl Bridenbaugh, *The Colonial
   Craftsman* (New York: New York University Press,
   1950), pp. 125-126, 128.

*development may be used to refer to broad cultural rather
than strictly religious characteristics.*

✔   ✔   ✔

These names of virtues, with their precepts, were:
1. TEMPERANCE. Eat not to dullness; drink not to
elevation; 2. SILENCE. Speak not but what may benefit
others or yourself; avoid trifling conversation; 3. ORDER.
Let all your things have their places; let each part of your
business have its time. 4. RESOLUTION. Resolve to perform what you ought; perform without fail what you resolve. 5. FRUGALITY. Make no expense but to do good
to others or yourself; *i.e.,* waste nothing. 6. INDUSTRY.
Lose no time; be always employ'd in something useful; cut
off all unnecessary actions. 7. SINCERITY. Use no hurt-
ful deceit; think innocently and justly, and, if you speak,
speak accordingly. 8. JUSTICE. Wrong none by doing in-
juries, or omitting the benefits that are your duty. 9.
MODERATION. Avoid extreams; forbear resenting in-
juries so much as you think they deserve. 10. CLEANLI-
NESS. Tolerate no uncleanliness in body, cloaths, or
habitation. 11. TRANQUILITY. Be not disturbed at tri-
fles, or at accidents common or unavoidable. 12. CHAS-
TITY. Rarely use venery but for health or offspring,
never to dulness, weakness, or the injury of your own or
another's peace or reputation. 13. HUMILITY. Imitate
Jesus and Socrates.

————————

II

*The varied character and seasonal rhythm of the mer-
chant's business are clear in an account of Thomas Hancock's store in Boston.*

✔   ✔   ✔

This store must have looked very like the general
dealer's shop in a small village today. It sold almost everything. But, though the Hancock's wares covered a wide
range, one class of goods was more important than all the
others put together—at least, such was the case from 1755
onwards, the period for which we have figures. If we split

up home sales into broad groups, we find what might be
called the dress department (including such things as
coarse cloth, ribbons, knee and show buckles, and fans)
comes an easy first; it accounts for two-thirds of the
total. Hardware (e.g., brass compasses, fire steels, hour
glasses, larding pins, and swords) lags a long way behind,
with some 10 per cent of the total; and provisions (with
rum) are a shade lower. Tea amounts to an extra 1 per
cent, while both coal and ships' stores are just under
this small fraction. Stationery and books are still given a
tiny corner in the store, but together make up only .6 per
cent of the sales. In addition to these lines (all handled
fairly regularly), about 10 per cent of the total consists of
big single transactions in salt, leather, lime, and so on.

There was a marked seasonal rhythm in the flow of
custom. Winter was a slack time. When the spring goods
arrived from London, there was an immediate spurt in
the number of sales, which nearly doubled; and, since
the size of the individual orders also increased, the volume
of goods sent out must have trebled between January and
April. By July, business was again dull. Then came the
fall orders, and another spurt followed till November.

In a town as small as Boston then was, the coming of
a boat from Britain was an event, and set the tempo for
business. When his spring or fall shipments arrived, a
trader would hasten to lure customers to his shop with
handbills or press advertisements stating that he had
"imported in the 'Hayley' from London A large and
general Assortment of Winter Goods which he will sell by
Wholesale and Retail at the lowest Rates for Cash."
Thomas believed in advertising in the papers fairly regularly, and he sometimes managed to inject a more vital
tang into his notices, e.g., "Excellent good Bohea Tea,
imported in the last ship from London: sold by Tho.
Hancock. N. B. If it don't suit the ladies' taste, they may
return the tea and receive their money again."

III

*The complexity of the overseas trade of merchants at
a mature stage of such enterprise is shown in a letter of*

*instructions from William Gray of Salem, a great eight-
eenth-century merchant, to his brother-in-law as captain
of a ship.*

Salem, August 9, 1792

Capt. William Ward,—

The Brig Enterprise under your command being ready
for sea, you will embrace the first opportunity and proceed for the Cape of Good Hope—upon your arrival sell
such part of the cargo as you can to advantage which
I suppose will be the Russia duck, coles and such other
part of your cargo as you think proper. I then advise you,
if you can, to purchase about twenty hogsheads of brandy
and from 60 to 80 hogsheads wine, such as is best calculated for the Isle of France market, some raisins and
almonds, and then proceed for the Isle of France, then
sell your cargo or such part as you think for my interest to
sell, which I expect will be the whole, when you have sold
if you can find any sugar, coffee, tea, Indigo, or cotton
that will pay one hundred per cent profitt reckoning them
to sell at the price you have at foot then I advise you to
come back with such of those articles as you find will
do best if you cannot find goods to answer to come home
from the Isle of France, then I advise you to proceed
for Calcutta in the Bay of Bengal, and there take sugar,
saltpeters, Bandanno silk Handkerchiefs, or such other
goods as you suppose will answer best in this market. If
you have advise that nothing can be done to advantage
at Calcutta then you may go to Canton if you can get a
cargo of Black wood, cheep, provided you can make out
a stock of $20,000, exclusive of Black wood. When you
arrive at Canton after selling your wood take on board
as much Bohea tea, as the Brig will carry with some
China ware, nankeens, some black sattins, and such other
silks as you suppose will best answer. When you have
compleated your business in the East Indies proceed directly to this port by such rout as you think safest, if you
should come home in the winter it may be well to touch
at St. Eustatia and then lay till the spring approaches, so
that you may come on safer. I think it may be well to
send your boat on shore of Triniti in Martinico where perhaps you will find letters from me. It will be best to sett

your cooper at work as soon as you possibly can, and to agree for your wines and Brandies as soon as you can after you arrive, your cargo will sell for 10 or 20 per cent more to take wines and brandies than cash.

Notwithstanding what I have wrote I would have you sell your whole cargo at Good Hope if you can obtain 20 per cent advance and purchase sugars or any other goods that will pay fifty per cent profit home, then proceed directly to this port. If you have opportunity to sell the Brig Enterprise and appurtanance at a price that you think will answer and can lay out the money to advantage, do it. She cost five thousand dollars and will be worth that surely when she returns, you will take into your calculations what freight she will make home what you must pay freight and what you can make profitt upon the proceeds of the Brig. . . .

Write me by all opportunities either to America or Europe. If to England, direct to the care of Messrs. Harrison Ansley & Co in London, if to Spain to Gardoqui & Co in Bilboa. If to France then to the care of Messrs. Lanchon & Co at L'Orient. If to Denmark to the care of Messrs. Ryberg & Co. at Copenhagen. If to Sweden then to the care of Mr. Thomas Erstein at Gottenburg. The port charges at Canton I suppose about three thousand dollars, at Calcutta the port charges are small. . . .

I further agree Captain Ward shall receive of the profitts that shall be made upon one hundred pound averaging my whole stock in this voyage at his return—as a further consideration for his services. In case you can obtain a credit to advantage and lay out the amount so as to pay me profitt you may take to the amount of six thousand dollars and draw upon me—payable either here or in London—and your bills shall meet due honour.

Wishing you Almighty protection and a prosperous voyage

I am your Friend
William Gray Jr.

Salem 10 August 1792.

IV

Here is a picture of an artisan's house and shop from the well-informed imagination of Carl Bridenbaugh.

✓   ✓   ✓

Walk with me in fancy along the north side of Market (High) Street in Philadelphia of 1772 at about eight o'clock on a bright morning in June. On our right the countryfolk have been astir in the market stalls and the tradesmen have been hard at work in their shops since before six and will remain there till darkness brings a close to their labors. . . .

Proceeding from this busy scene to the corner of Second Street, we now turn north . . . as far as Vine, we enter the pewterer's shop of William Will, which is both wholesale and retail. His wife and daughter take down from the shelves for our inspection several pewter basins, flagons, mugs, tankards, and plates, either imported from London or made by the proprietor. Next we go into a small building to the rear of the shop to watch the men at work. Mr. Will is seated before a bench assembling the several parts of a tankard; an apprentice wearily cranks the great wheel that turns the lathe at which one of the master's sons is polishing a napkin ring; another apprentice is rolling a plate mould as he pours in the hot metal; and over by the forge a journeyman is carefully pouring pewter into a small mould, a task requiring all his skill. . . .

Professor Bridenbaugh reports on the capital needed by craftsmen.

✓   ✓   ✓

An artisan just starting out for himself did not need to make a large investment; tools and materials were not costly. Of the hundreds of occupations practiced at London in 1747 it was estimated that eight required £5 "to set up a master"; ten needed £10; twenty-five needed £20; ninetey needed £50; and seventy-five needed £100. In present-day values this means that $150 to

$2500 would be sufficient capital for a man to enter a trade, purchase tools and stock, and maintain himself until he completed his work for sale. The amounts would have been about the same in the colonies.

— Reading No. 3 —

THE REVOLUTIONARY ERA[3]

I

In a period of new imperial policies, armed rebellion against them, and the formation of new states, the most interesting contemporary views are concerned with the relations of business and government. British merchants disliked the new tax policies of the 1760's almost as much as did Americans. This extract from a petition to the House of Commons from the merchants of London in 1766 reflects their opposition to imperial policy and summarizes the conditions of the British export trade to the North American colonies.

That the petitioners have been long concerned in carrying on the trade between this country and the British colonies on the continent of North America; and that they have annually exported very large quantities of British manufactures, consisting of woolen goods of all kinds,

[3] For I, Petition of London Merchants against the Stamp Act, January 17, 1766, from *The Parliamentary History of England*, Vol. XVI, pp. 133ff. For II, The Association, October 20, 1774, *Journals of the Continental Congress*, ed. W. C. Ford, Vol. I, pp. 75ff. For III, Diary of Benjamin Rush in the Philadelphia, Pa., Free Library, Ridgway Branch.

cottons, linens, hardware, shoes, household furniture, and almost without exception of every other species of goods manufactured in these kingdoms, besides other articles imported from abroad, chiefly purchased with our manufactures and with the produce of our colonies; by all which, many thousand manufacturers, seamen and labourers, have been employed, to the very great and increasing benefit of this nation; and that, in return for these exports, the petitioners have received from the colonies, rice, indigo, tobacco, naval stores, oil, whale fins, furs, and lately potash, with other commodities, besides remittances by bills of exchange and bullion, obtained by the colonists in payment for articles of their produce, not required for the British market, and therefore exported to other places; and that, from the nature of this trade, consisting of British manufactures exported, and of the import of raw materials from America, many of them used in our manufactures, and all of them tending to lessen our dependence on neighboring states, it must be deemed of the highest importance in the commercial system of this nation; and that this commerce, so beneficial to the state, and so necessary for the support of multitudes, now lies under such difficulties and discouragement, that nothing less than its utter ruin is apprehended, without the immediate interposition of parliament; and that, in consequence of the trade between the colonies and the mother country, as established and as permitted for many years, and of the experience which the petitioners have had of the readiness of the Americans to make their just remittances to the utmost of their real ability, they have been induced to make and venture such large exportations of British manufactures, as to leave the colonies indebted to the merchants of Great Britain in the sum of several millions sterling; and that at this time the colonists, when pressed for payment, appeal to past experience, in proof of their willingness; but declare it is not in their power, at present, to make good their engagements, alleging, that the taxes and restrictions laid upon them, and the extension of the jurisdiction of vice admiralty courts established by some late acts of parliament . . . have so far interrupted the usual and former most fruitful branches of their commerce, restrained the sale of their produce, thrown the

state of the several provinces into confusion, and brought
on so great a number of actual bankruptcies, that the
former opportunities and means of remittances and payments are utterly lost and taken from them. . . .

II

*A chief weapon of Americans in combating British
revenue laws was the nonimportation agreements signed
by merchants in each major port. Apparent success in
1765 and 1768 in producing modification in British regulations gave Americans considerable confidence in the
coercive power of such agreements. Consequently, when
the British Coercive Acts of 1774 placed intolerable
burdens on the people of Massachusetts, their representatives were able to get the delegates to a Continental Congress to agree to use not only nonimportation but also the
threat of nonexportation as their chief methods of exerting
pressure on the Tory ministry in London. Section 11 of
the nonimportation "Association," however, went one
step further than earlier agreements in setting up committees for enforcement. These committees became the
nuclei of revolutionary political organizations which were
in general hostile toward merchants. Thus, while the merchants had entered nonimportation rather willingly in the
depression of 1765, and half-heartedly in 1768, the Association of 1774 was forced upon them, against the will of
the majority of the more substantial traders, by ardent
revolutionary patriots.*

We, his majesty's most loyal subjects, the delegates of
the several colonies . . . in a continental Congress, held
in the city of Philadelphia, on the 5th day of September,
1774, avowing our allegiance to his majesty, our affection
and regard for our fellow-subjects in Great-Britain and
elsewhere, affected with the deepest anxiety, and most
alarming apprehensions, at those grievances and distresses,
with which his Majesty's American subjects are oppressed;
and having taken under our most serious deliberation, the
state of the whole continent, find, that the present unhappy
situation of our affairs is occasioned by a ruinous system

of colony administration, adopted by the British ministry about the year 1763, evidently calculated for enslaving these colonies, and with them, the British empire. . . .

To obtain redress of these grievances, which threaten destruction to the lives, liberty, and property of his majesty's subjects, in North-America, we are of the opinion, that a non-importation, non-consumption, and non-exportation agreement, faithfully adhered to, will prove the most speedy, effectual, and peaceable measure: And, therefore, we do, for ourselves, and the inhabitants of the several colonies, whom we represent, firmly agree and associate, under the sacred ties of virtue, honour and love of our country, as follows:

1. That from and after the first day of December next, we will not import, into British America from Great-Britain or Ireland, any goods, wares, or merchandize whatsoever, or from any other place, any such goods, wares, or merchandize, as shall have been exported from Great-Britain or Ireland; nor will we, after that day, import any East-India tea from any part of the world; nor any molasses, syrups, paneles, coffee, or pimento, from the British plantations or from Dominica; nor wines from Madeira, or the Western Islands; nor foreign indigo.

2. We will neither import nor purchase, any slave imported after the first day of December next; after which time, we will wholly discontinue the slave trade, and will neither be concerned in it ourselves, nor will we hire our vessels, nor sell our commodities or manufactures to those concerned in it.

3. As a non-consumption agreement, strictly adhered to, will be an effectual security for the observation of the non-importation, we, as above, solemnly agree and associate, that from this day, we will not purchase or use any tea, imported on account of the East-India company, or any on which a duty hath been or shall be paid; and from and after the first day of March next, we will not purchase or use any of those goods, wares, or merchandize, we have agreed not to import, which we shall know, or have cause to suspect, were imported after the first day of December, except such as come under the rules and directions of the tenth article hereafter named.

4. The earnest desire we have not to injure our fellow-

subjects in Great Britain, Ireland, or the West-Indies, induces us to suspend a non-exportation, until the tenth day of September, 1775; at which time, if the said acts and parts of acts of the British parliament herein mentioned, are not repealed, we will not directly or indirectly, export any merchandize or commodity whatsoever to Great-Britain, Ireland, or the West-Indies, except rice to Europe.

5. Such as are merchants, and use the British and Irish trade, will give orders, as soon as possible, to their factors, agents and correspondents, in Great-Britain and Ireland, not to ship any goods to them, on any pretence whatsoever, as they cannot be received in America; and if any merchant residing in Great-Britain or Ireland, shall directly or indirectly ship any goods, wares or merchandize, for America, in order to break the said non-importation agreement, or in any manner contravene the same, on such unworthy conduct being well attested, it ought to be made public; and, on the same being so done, we will not, from thenceforth, have any commercial connexion with such merchant. . . .

III

In addition to interruptions of trade brought about by the war, mercantile business was harassed after 1776 by rapidly depreciating state and Continental currency, and by efforts in some states to fix prices at levels below those of the market. At the end of 1776, after the four New England states had drawn up price fixing resolutions, a resolution was introduced in the Continental Congress to urge all states to do likewise. The arguments against the resolution illustrate the merchants' point of view, although their most eloquent champion was Dr. Rush, the famous Philadelphia physician.

✓   ✓   ✓

Dr. Rush: I am against the whole of the resolution. It is founded in the contrary of justice, policy and necessity as has been declared in the resolution. The wisdom and power of government have been employed in all ages to regulate the price of necessaries to no purpose. It was attempted in England in the reign of Edward II by the

English parliament, but without effect. The laws for limiting the price of everything were repealed, and Mr. Hume who mentions this fact records even the very attempt as a monument of human folly.

The Congress with all its authority has failed in a former instance of regulating the price of goods. You have limited Bohea tea to ¾ of a dollar, and yet it is daily sold before your eyes for 30s. The Committee of Philadelphia limited the price of West India goods about a year ago. But what was the consequence? The merchants, it is true, sold their rum, sugar and molasses at the price limited by the committee, but they charged a heavy profit upon the barrel, or the paper which contained the rum or the sugar. . . .

It is a common thing to cry aloud of the rapacity and extortion in every branch of business, etc., among every class of men. This has led some people to decry the *public virtue* of this country. We estimate our virtue by a false barometer when we measure it by the price of goods. The extortion we complain of arises only from the excessive quantity of money. Now, Sir, a failure in this attempt to regulate the price of goods will encrease the clamors against the rapacity of dealers, and thus depreciate our public virtue.

Consider, Sir, the consequence of measuring our virtue by this false standard. You will add weight to the arguments used at St. James's to explode patriotism altogether, and by denying its existence in this country destroy it forever. Persuade a woman that there is no such thing as chastity, and, if there is, that she does not possess it, and she may be easily seduced if she was as chaste as Diana. Sir, the price of goods may be compared to a number of light substances in a bason of water. The hand may keep them down for a while, but nothing can detain them on the bottom of the bason but an abstraction of the water. The continent labours under a universal malady. From the crown of her head to the soles of her feet she is full of disorders. She requires the most powerful tonic medicines. The resolution before you is nothing but an opiate. It may compose the continent for a night, but she will soon awaken again to a fresh sense of her pain and misery.

— Reading No. 4 —

THE CORPORATION[4]

I

Corporate charters were lengthy documents that cannot be reproduced here. The following sections from the Charter of the Bank of New York in 1791 illustrate typical language and provisions. A number of other early charters had voting arrangements at variance with the later practice of one vote for each share. While this Charter is specified as that of a bank and certain other activities are forbidden to the company, there is no effort to define banking or to set up rules for its operation.

I. *Be it enacted by the People of the State of New York, represented in Senate and Assembly, and it is hereby enacted by the authority of the same,* That all such persons as now are, or hereafter shall be, stockholders of the said bank, shall be, and hereby are, ordained, constituted, and declared to be, from time to time, and until the second Tuesday of May, which will be in the year one thousand eight hundred and eleven, a body corporate and politic, in fact and in name, by the name of the President, Directors, and Company of the Bank of New York . . .

[4] For I, An Act to Incorporate the Stockholders of the Bank of New York, Passed March 21, 1791, as quoted in Henry W. Domett, *A History of the Bank of New York* (New York: G. P. Putnam's Sons, 1884), pp. 122-130. For II, Laws of New York 1811, Chap. 27.

II. *And be it further enacted by the authority afore-said,* That a share in the stock of the said bank shall be five hundred Spanish milled dollars, or the equivalent thereof in specie. . . .

III. *And be it further enacted by the authority afore-said,* That the stock, property, affairs, and concerns of the said corporation shall be managed and conducted by thirteen directors, one of whom to be the President, who shall hold their offices for one year, which directors shall be stockholders, and shall be citizens of this State, and be elected on the second Tuesday of May in every year, at such time of the day, and at such place in the city of New York, as a majority of the directors, for the time being, shall appoint; and public notice shall be given by the said directors, in two of the newspapers printed in said city, of such time and place, not more than twenty nor less than ten days previous to the time of holding the said election; and the said election shall be held and made by such of the said stockholders of the said bank as shall attend for that purpose, in their own proper persons or by proxy; and all elections for directors shall be by ballot, and the thirteen persons who shall have the greatest number of votes at any election shall be the directors, except as hereinafter directed. . . .

V. *And be it further enacted by the authority aforesaid,* That each stockholder shall be entitled to a number of votes proportioned to the number of shares which he or she shall have held in his or her own name at least three months prior to the time of voting, according to the following ratios—that is to say, at the rate of one vote for each share not exceeding four, five votes for six shares, six votes for eight shares, seven votes for ten shares, and one vote for every five shares above ten; stockholders actually resident within the United States, and none other, may vote in elections by proxy. . . .

VII. *And be it further enacted by the authority afore-said,* That the directors for the time being, or a major part of them, shall have power to make and prescribe such by-laws, rules, and regulations as to them shall appear needful and proper, touching the management and disposition of the stock, property, estate, and effects of the said corporation, and touching the duties and conduct of the officers, clerks, and servants employed therein, and touching the election of directors, and all such other matters as appertain to the business of a bank. . . .

VIII. *And be it further enacted by the authority of aforesaid,* That this State shall have a right to subscribe any number of shares to the said bank, not exceeding in the whole the number of one hundred, at any time when they shall by law authorize any person or persons for that purpose. . . .

II

A general incorporation act was a law setting up a charter with standard provisions which incorporators could secure by application to a state commissioner. The provisions of the first such general act for manufacturing companies, passed in New York in 1811, indicates by their simplicity how much of the practice of corporations was already a matter of legal precedents which did not need to be repeated in each charter.

✔   ✔   ✔

AN EARLY GENERAL INCORPORATION LAW

An act relative to incorporations for manufacturing purposes. Passed March 29, 1811.

1. *Be it enacted by the people of the State of New York represented in Senate and Assembly,* That at any time within five years hereafter, any five or more persons who shall be desirous to form a company for the purpose of manufacturing woolen, cotton or linen goods, or for the purpose of making glass, or for the purpose of making ore from bar-iron, anchor, mill irons, steel, nail rods, hoop iron and iron mongery, sheet copper, sheet lead, shot, white lead and red lead may make, sign and acknowledge, before a justice of the Supreme Court, a judge of the Court of Common Pleas, or a master in Chancery, and file in the office of the Secretary of State a certificate in writing in which shall be stated the corporate name of the said company, and the objects for which the company is formed, the amount of the capital stock of the said company, the number of shares of which the said stock shall consist, the number of trustees

and their names who shall manage the concerns of the said company for the first year and the names of the town and county in which the manufacturing operations of the said company are to be carried on.

2. *And be it further enacted,* That as soon as such certificate shall be filed as foresaid, the persons who shall have signed and acknowledged the said certificate and their successors, shall for the term of twenty years next after the day of filing such certificate, be a body corporate and politic, in fact and name, by the name stated in such certificate, and by that name they and their successors shall and may have continual succession, and shall be persons in law capable of suing and being sued, pleading and being impleaded, answering or being answered unto, defending and being defended, in all courts and places whatsoever, in all manner of actions, suits, complaints, matters and causes whatsoever; and they and their successors may have a common seal, and the same may make, alter and change at their pleasure, and that they and their successors, by their corporate name, shall in law be capable of buying, purchasing, holding and conveying any lands, tenements, hereditaments, goods, wares and merchandise whatsoever necessary to enable the said company to carry on their manufacturing operations mentioned in such certificate.

3. *And be it further enacted,* That the stock, property and concerns of such company shall be managed and conducted by trustees, who, except for those for the first year, shall be elected at such time and place as shall be directed by the law of said company, and public notice shall be given of the time and place of holding such election, not less than ten days previous thereto, in the newspaper printed nearest to the place where the manufacturing operations of the said company shall or are to be carried on, and the election shall be made by such stockholders as shall attend for that purpose, either in person or by proxy, and all elections shall be by ballot, and each stockholder shall be entitled to as many votes as he owns shares of stock of the said company, and the persons having the greatest number of votes shall be trustees and whenever any vacancy shall happen among trustees by death, resignation or removal out of the State,

such vacancy shall be filled for the remainder of the year in such manner as shall be provided by the laws of the said company; *Provided always, That* the number of trustees shall not exceed nine, and that they shall respectively be stockholders in such company.

4. *And be it further enacted,* That in case it shall at any time happen that an election of trustees be not made on the day when by the by-laws of the said company it ought to have been done, the said company for that cause shall not be dissolved, but it shall and may be lawful on any other day to hold an election for trustees, in such manner as shall be subscribed by the by-laws of such company.

5. *And be it further enacted,* That the capital stock of such company shall not exceed one hundred thousand dollars; and it shall be lawful for the trustees to call and demand from the stockholders respectively all such sums of money by them subscribed at such times and in such proportions as they shall deem proper, under pain of forfeiting the shares of the said stockholders and all previous payments made thereon, if such payments shall not be made, within sixty days after a notice requiring such payment shall have been published in such newspaper as aforesaid. . . .

— Reading No. 5 —

EARLY BANKING [5]

I

Edmond John Forstall of New Orleans, merchant, planter, and banker, was influential in framing a banking law for Louisiana in 1842 that was a model for early banking practices. In a letter written to the Directors of the Citizens' Bank, of which he was president in 1838, he outlined the proper management of a bank.

The duties devolving upon the president of a property bank carry with them a responsibility of no ordinary magnitude: the fortunes of thousands of families depend upon the good or bad management of the directory over which he presides; he is, by law, the immediate guardian of the property of the bank; he must see that the affairs of the bank are carried on according to the true intent and meaning of the act of corporation; that expediency be not preferred to principles; that the rules laid down for the guidance of the bank be not encroached upon; that the money borrowed on the property of the stockholders be

[5] For I, U. S. 25th Cong. 3rd sess., *House Executive Document,* 227, p. 564, as quoted in Fritz Redlich, *The Molding of American Banking: Men and Ideas,* Part II (New York: Hafner Publishing Co.), pp. 33, 38. For II, as quoted in Bray Hammond, *Banks and Politics in America from the Revolution to the Civil War* (Princeton: Princeton University Press, 1957), p. 553; and George D. Lyman, "Bank Exchanges," *New York Journal of Commerce,* November 21, 1851, as quoted in Redlich, *American Banking,* p. 49.

loaned out upon at least equal security; that the guaranty
of one stockholder should not be lessened at the expense
of another; that the guaranty of the State and bond-holders
be held sacred; that the bank abstain from using her deposits, unless fully prepared to meet them under all circumstances; that the other business of the bank be at all
times made subservient to her functions as an issuer of
currency; he must watch closely the domestic and foreign
exchanges, that he may know when to expand, when to
contract: in fine, his supervision and correspondence
must embrace the whole sphere of action of the
bank. . . .

First. Hereafter the loans of the bank shall be distributed as follows:

1. Loans on stocks, as required by the charter.
2. Loans on business paper, i.e., paper on personal
   security, payable at full maturity.
3. Loans on accommodation paper, to be guaranteed
   by mortgage on real estate, and not to exceed
   two-thirds of the cash value of said estate.

Second. The bank shall hold, at all times, an amount
of business paper, maturing within sixty days, equal to
the amount of its deposits and circulation; every note
secured by personal security shall be, *de facto,* considered
as business paper; and every note secured by mortgage
shall be considered as accommodation paper.

Third. No renewal of business paper shall take place,
unless forced by extraordinary circumstances; and in all
such cases, the maker or endorser of such paper shall be
required to give a mortgage on real estate; and the paper
thus secured and no other, shall be considered as accommodation paper.

Fourth. The operations of the bank shall be conducted
in such a manner as to discount an equal amount of
accommodation paper for the country and the city. Country accommodations shall be made payable from February
to April, and shall be renewable, if required, on the payment of a per centum equal to the number of months for
which the loan shall have been made, multiplied by five.
The city accommodations shall be made payable at four
months, and renewable on the payment of twenty per
cent.

Fifth. The cashier on each discount day shall lay before the board a statement showing—

1. Loans to stockholders.
2. Loans on accommodation, under the heads of 'city' and 'country,' and when due.
3. Loans on business paper, when due.
4. Cash responsibilities of the bank. . . .

II

The development of workable principles for the operation of individual commercial banks still left the problem of "clearing" checks and notes untouched. As stated in the text, the Suffolk Bank of Boston established an unformalized clearing association for country bank notes in the 1820's. Some of the difficulties of operating such a system without legal support are indicated in this statement issued by the Suffolk in 1836 to certain country banks.

In consequence of the great increase of banks in the New England states during the past winter, and the scarcity of specie, it has become impracticable to allow any further overdrafts on this bank, or to hold your bills beyond the amount of funds to your credit. Your account is now overdrawn __________ dollars, which we must rely upon your making good with as little delay as possible; and we shall be compelled to send your bills home for specie in the future, unless you have funds here to redeem them. We regret the necessity of these measures, but the deranged state of money matters throughout our whole country renders them unavoidable.

The movement for organized clearing houses succeeded in the 1850's. The use and advantages of such a device were described in an article in the Journal of Commerce *by George D. Lyman in 1851.*

Let the banks select some one bank as a medium for exchanging, to be the Exchange Bank of the city, and let an account be kept by all the city banks with this bank alone; each bank assorting and making up its exchanges as now, but all the banks sending their gross amount of exchanges to the bank so selected, at some regular hour in the morning of each day. . . . The entire amount of exchanges would thus be brought together and would soon be distributed with but little more labor than each bank is now subject to, made up with a slip of the Exchanging bank, which would be footed. . . . They should then meet at some regular hour . . . at the Exchange Bank to receive from it any checks returned not good and for the correcting of any errors that may have been discovered. . . . Balances should be settled as now. Debtor banks should be required to pay up once a week, or every day . . . In this way the number of balances would be greatly reduced and specie would . . . stay longer in one place.

✓ Reading No. 6 —

EARLY MANUFACTURING[6]

I

In the young republic, trying to establish itself in a world continuously upset by war, investment in manufacturing became a patriotic duty. At a dinner in Philadelphia in 1808, during the Embargo on foreign trade, David Humphries proposed a toast: "The Best Mode of Warfare for our Country—the artillery of carding and spinning machinery, and the musketry of shuttles and sledges." (Samuel Reyneck, "The Rise and Early Development of Industrial Consciousness in the United States," The Journal of Economic and Business History, IV, p. 801).

In 1794 Tench Coxe, Assistant Secretary of the Treas-

---

[6] For I, Tench Coxe, *A View of the United States of America* (Philadelphia, 1794), pp. 38-39, 42, 443; and C. W. Janson, *Stranger in America* (London, 1807), pp. 195-196. For II, Thomas C. Cochran, *The Pabst Brewing Company, The History of an American Business* (New York: New York University Press, 1948), pp. 20-21. For III, William Tudor, *Letters on Eastern States* (Boston, 1821), p. 266, and as quoted from John E. Sawyer, "The American System of Manufacturing," *The Journal of Economic History* XIV, 4 (1954), pp. 378, 374, 372. For IV, Theodore Marburg, "Imperfect Competition in Brass Manufacturing During the 1830's," *The Journal of Economic History,* Supplement III (December, 1943), pp. 34-35; and Victor S. Clark, *History of Manufactures in the United States* (New York: McGraw-Hill, 1929), Vol. I, p. 458.

ury, wrote a book on the economic prospects of the United States in which he explained how industry could arise, alongside agriculture. He also correctly emphasized the importance of immigration in supplying skilled workers and managers.

✔   ✔   ✔

Factories which can be carried on by water-mills, wind-mills, fire, horses and machines ingeniously contrived, are not burdened with any heavy expense of boarding, lodging, clothing and paying workmen, and they supply the force of hands to a great extent without taking our people from agriculture. By wind and water machines we can make pig and bar iron, nail rods, tire, sheet-iron, sheet-copper, sheet-brass, anchors, meal of all kinds, gun-powder, writing, and hanging paper, snuff, linseed oil, boards, plank and scantling; and they assist us in finish-ing scythes, sickles and woolen cloths. Strange as it may appear they also card, spin and even weave, it is said, by water in the European factories. Bleaching and tan-ning must not be omitted, we shall probably see them after a short time in places, where there are few mill seats in this and other great towns of the United States. . . . The blessings of civil and religious liberty in America, and the oppressions of most foreign governments, the want of employment at home and the expectations of profit here, curiosity, domestic unhappiness, civil war and various other circumstances will bring many manufac-turers to this asylum for mankind. . . . A large propor-tion of the most successful manufacturers in the United States are persons, who were journeymen, and in a few instances were foremen in the work-shops and manufac-tories of Europe, who having been skilfull, sober and frugal, and having thus saved a little money, have set up for themselves with great advantage in America.

Starting with the Pennsylvania Society for the En-couragement of Manufactures and Useful Arts in 1787, many associations, incorporated and unincorporated, were formed to aid manufacturing. Some, such as the one of

1805 described below, were prepared to invest money in a part of the process of manufacturing and selling.

✓   ✓   ✓

In Philadelphia and the adjacent towns a considerable quantity of stockings are made, and other small manufactures carried on. But for want of a regular demand, the manufacturers are obliged to attend the market twice a week. Thus they lose one third of their time in endeavoring to sell what they make in the other two thirds. This is not the greatest hardship under which they labor. The contempt shown to domestic manufacture . . . obliges him to make great sacrifices. Thus this industrious part of the community too often comes to poverty and distress.

A few patriotic individuals have lately associated themselves for the purpose of assisting these unfortunate people. They propose an application to the legislature for a charter to incorporate a company for encouraging the sale of American manufactures, of woolen, cotton, and linen. The funds of the proposed company are to arise from a subscription of one hundred dollars each. . . . A warehouse is to be opened for the reception of finished and marketable goods of the above-mentioned fabrics, where the articles shall be deposited at the makers' prices. They are then to be inspected by competent judges of the commodities, who shall say how much, in their judgment, they ought to sell for. The company are then to advance one half in cash on the amount of the price fixed, and the other half when the goods are sold, subject to a very small deduction, to form a fund, from which, after subtracting the expenses of the establishment, the profits or interest on the capital will arise. . . . The owners of goods left for sale at the warehouse may at any time withdraw them, on repaying the money advanced and the expenses incurred; and all goods that may remain unsold, and which the owner will not redeem, shall be sold at auction at stated periods, and if more shall be received for them than the money advanced, and the charges, the surplus shall be paid to the owner of the goods.

II

*Most American manufacturing companies were started
with too little capital and its corollary inadequate equipment. An account, from memory, of one aspect of the
founding of Best, later Pabst, brewery gives much of the
atmosphere of pioneer industry.*

✓   ✓   ✓

In the summer of the year mentioned (1844) Phillip
(Best) who was the businessman of the firm, came to my
office on the canal, and asked me to make him a steam
boiler to be used in the manufacture of "Lager Beer." I
told him that I was familiar with their construction, it
being a part of my business while in New York, but
I disliked very much to have the noisy things around, and
did not wish to do so. After considerable urging however
I consented to make it, as I found a machinist in my
employ used to riveting. I could only find two sheets of
boiler iron in Milwaukee and went to Racine and Kenosha
who were then in earnest rivalry with us, as to a metropolitan seat on the Lake Shore, each declaiming their
superior advantages over each other, and over Milwaukee,
a village in the swamp, which never could be filled. Both
Racine and Kenosha were as sanguine as young roosters before their first defeat, and it is laughable to contrast the situation today. From Kenosha I went to Chicago and in all
four of these towns there was not enough iron to make a
single section of the boiler. On my way home with Captain Walker, one of the old time Sidewheeler Captains,
I made arrangements with him to get the iron for me in
Buffalo and on his return he did so, and in four weeks
thereafter the boiler was ready for delivery. I planned its
construction and helped do the riveting, mainly done on
the dock out of doors, and the inhabitants of Milwaukee
hearing the music of riveting all came to see it and I
think if the roll had been called at that time that every
man, woman, and child except the invalids, would have
answered "here." It was the first boiler made in the
territory of Wisconsin, four years before she was admitted
to statehood. . . . When the boiler was completed Phillip
came with a red handkerchief loaded with various coins

taken in his business, which I think it took more time than an hour to count, and proved a great deal less than the amount due. At that time credit was unknown, all goods were spot cash. I could see that Phillip was dejected and in trouble. He said, "I had made the arrangement and had the promise of some money today on a mortgage of the premises where the boiler was going, but was disappointed. The man could not raise the money. I will leave the boiler until I can make enough money to pay the balance." I said to him, "Phillip, take the boiler, get to work as soon as possible and pay as soon as you can conveniently." He had not expected this and dare not ask it. I may say that he was filled with great joy, and ever after my most ardent friend.

III

Substitution of machinery for labor whenever possible has been a dominant interest of American industrial management from the early days of the factory processes. This was evident in 1820 from one of the writings by William Tudor on eastern manufacturing.

There are no people more ingenious in the use and invention of machinery, no country more prolific in patents, than the one under consideration. Good mechanics are to be found in every one of the mechanic arts, and the improvements they have made in some old, and the invention of many new instruments, are strong proofs of their skill and enterprise. These are not shown merely in the common tools in use in various trades, but in the most complicated and useful machines. Such, for instance, are the card and nail machines, which are so extensively used in the United States. These are entirely of their own invention. They have also improved the machines used in Europe, in the process of spinning and weaving; —though the machinery was considered almost perfect there, they have made many ameliorations. In this department, also, we have an advantage over the European manufacturer;—no resistance is made here to the introduction of any machinery; every kind of labour-saving machine is eagerly sought after, and new ones are constantly coming into use. In Europe, the manufacturer is often limited in this respect; he is often afraid to make use of machinery that would be of essential service to him. Machinery that is used in one country, sometimes cannot be brought into another, without producing a riot among the workmen. Within a few years the most serious mischief, alarming and long continued disturbances, have arisen from this source. Our manufacturers have no fears of this kind to encounter.

By the 1850's the British were so impressed by "the American system of manufacture" that they sent men over to investigate it and report to Parliament. The following excerpts from reports in 1853 and 1854 provide a reliable view of how the attitudes and practices of American workers and managers differed from those of England.

As there is no apprenticeship system, properly so called, the more useful the youth engaged in any industrial pursuit becomes to his employer, the more profitable it is for himself. Bringing a mind prepared by thorough school discipline, and educated up to a far higher standard than those of a much superior social grade in society in the Old World, the American working boy develops rapidly into the skilled artizan, and having once mastered one part of his business, he is never content until he has mastered all. . . . The restless activity of mind and body —the anxiety to improve his own department of industry —the facts constantly before him of ingenious men who have solved economic and mechanical problems to their own profit and elevation, are all stimulative and encouraging; and it may be said that there is not a working boy of average ability in the New England states, at least, who has not an idea of some mechanical invention or improvement in manufactures, by which, in good time, he hopes to better his position, or rise to fortune and social distinction.

On this intelligent understanding of the true position of things, and the requirements of the social system around him, the skilled workman rests his position. . . .

As regards the class of machinery usually employed by engineers and machine makers, they [the Americans] are upon the whole behind those of England, but in the adaptation of special apparatus to a single operation in almost all branches of industry, the Americans display an amount of ingenuity, combined with undaunted energy, which as a nation we would do well to imitate, if we mean to hold our present position in the great market of the world.

The Committee also observed that everything that could be done to reduce labour in the movement of materials from one point to another was adopted. This includes mechanical arrangements for lifting material, &c., from one floor to another, carriages for conveying material on the same floor, and such like.

Many of the parts . . . are polished on buffs, in the same manner as practiced in England; but on the whole less attention is bestowed on . . . high finish given to the parts, only to please the eye.

IV

High inland transportation costs before 1850 kept much industrial competition local or regional rather than nation-wide. Varying aspects of early competition are discussed in the following sections written by twentieth-century historians.

✦   ✦   ✦

In the 1830's there were four large producers manufacturing buttons, three of them located in the Naugatuck Valley of Connecticut, one located in Massachusetts. It is difficult to determine the degree to which price stability over any given period reflected a condition of oligopoly in equilibrium or a condition of price maintenance by gentleman's agreement. The Scovill brothers knew very well that any price reduction they made might call forth reductions on the part of their competitors. There were repeated intervals during which the manufacturers did come to agreement. . . .

Efforts to check price competition in selling buttons

were only partially and intermittently successful. They did have the effect that the seller oriented his thinking in terms of improvements or variations in his product which would increase sales and which would serve to distinguish his buttons from buttons in general. Such variations were sought in novel or timely patterns. In 1828 there were planished buttons, in 1830 buttons with flexible eyes. The next year a Henry Clay button sold well. In 1833 there were "Nullification" buttons for the South Carolinians. The first manufacturer to produce these items found the market his own because he had filled a unique and specialized demand. . . .

The rolling of sheet brass for sale was an outcome of the attempt to improve the quality of buttons. There were two domestic concerns producing sheet brass in the 1820's and a third concern started in the 1830's. Price competition was held in check intermittently during the 1830's, and in 1841 the procedure for establishing prices was regularized. A meeting of brass manufacturers assembled and drew up prices on each of various types of brass. By 1853 price agreement was well established and by 1856 output control was also instituted.

Competition took other forms than price reduction. Even in the case of sheet brass, seemingly so standard an item, there was opportunity for the manufacturer to differentiate his product. Quality determined reputation and reputation determined sales, hence flaws in the brass were to be kept at a minimum expressly to obtain the goodwill of customers. Personal calls on customers made it possible to generate goodwill and to supply a product peculiarly suited to the needs of each customer.

Two important New England [textile] manufacturing towns, Lowell and Fall River, were controlled by single companies and their allies, and their managers discouraged, if they did not prevent, the establishment at those places of independent competitors. Shortly after 1820 an attempt was made by the Taunton Manufacturing Company similarly to monopolize the industrial activities of that city, but without success. The Amoskeag Company, at Manchester, assimilated two neighboring companies by purchasing them, issuing for their stock its own stock in exchange. For several years close community of interests existed between the power and manufacturing companies at Lawrence and those at Lowell. In Rhode Island and southeastern Massachusetts wealthy mill-owning families like the Slaters, then the Spragues, and more recently the Knights and Bordens, acquired control of groups of factories, which they welded under their personal management into great aggregations of related industries directed by a common policy. Somewhat later dominant mill families arose in the cotton-spinning districts of the Carolinas.

These alliances and amalgamations never became monopolies and were not effective as price-fixing agencies. The agreement among the first cotton-spinners in Rhode Island to regulate the price of yarn, to which Moses Brown refers in his correspondence, and a later attempt of northern manufacturers of flannel to depress quotations at certain seasons in order to discourage importations, are the only specific attempts to regulate textile prices of which we have knowledge. . . .

— Reading No. 7 —

EARLY RETAILING[7]

I

Selling to a widely dispersed farm population was a major problem of early marketing. Yet even the frontiersman on the outposts of settlement needed guns, ammunition, knives, hoes, shoes, and countless other items that he could not make himself. Hence the peddler and the storekeeper went with the hunter and farmer to the frontier. The transition from wilderness to market town, from peddler to country store, is illustrated in this section from the work of Lewis E. Atherton.

If population was extremely scattered or too poor to buy in any quantity, the peddler by going from house to house and by covering a relatively large territory was able to operate, whereas more settled types of mercantile activity would have failed. Similarly, the artisan or custom-order worker took to the road when patronage was limited. An early-day settler of Jefferson County, Mississippi, recalled such men in his reminiscences. Jonathan Smallwood, an itinerant shoemaker, visited each family in late summer or early fall and remained until a new supply of

[7] For I, Lewis E. Atherton, *The Southern Country Store 1800-1860* (Baton Rouge: Louisiana State University Press, 1949), p. 167. For II, Herbert Barber Howe, *Jedediah Barber Howe, 1787-1876* (New York: Columbia University Press, 1939), pp. 55-56. For III, Atherton, *The Southern Country Store*, p. 21.

shoes had been provided for the whole family from hides saved during the past months. John Christy, a silversmith, operated in the same way, making silver spoons and cups for customers from Spanish-milled dollars.

When storekeepers entered such communities they compensated for the limited nature of the market by diversifying their economic activities. If they were successful in their efforts a village or town often developed. For example, Magnus S. Teague of Virginia was responsible for the growth of the village of Bluff Springs in Attala County, Mississippi. In 1823 he opened a general store in connection with a ferry across Big Black River. Teague also operated a sawmill, a gristmill, and a distillery. As the community developed he provided a post office, schoolhouse, Masonic-lodge building, blacksmith shop, church, and a site for a cemetery from his neighboring landholdings. Similarly, Huntsville in Montgomery County, Mississippi, developed from the store, saloon, and tenpin alley which Wilson Hunt established in 1844. In addition to these activities Hunt engaged in farming and operated a distillery to provide liquor for his saloon.

II

The general store tended to become the community center for news, reading, and conversation. The store brought eastern and European civilization to the wilderness, and prevented the loss of these cultural traditions. Herbert Barber Howe writes of his ancestor who kept an upstate New York store in the early nineteenth century.

⚹   ⚹   ⚹

In that day village storekeeping carried a prestige almost like that of a profession. The general store was the source of supply for all the wants of the people, excepting the products of the farm. And those very products were taken by the merchant in exchange for cloth, hardware, liquor, and good luxuries such as tea, coffee, sugar, and spices. In turn, the merchant had to sell at Albany

(from Homer, New York) the goods taken in barter—
grain and butter, meat and hides, as well as the products
of hand looms. And withal he was village banker, with a
keen knowledge of the affairs of each of his customers.
Finally, the merchant-trader must hold the confidence
and esteem of the people—must lead in public spirit in
those community affairs that united people. The minister
and physician had inherent authority to direct men and
women; the politician had a seasonal task as regards
affability; but the merchant must hold month in and
month out the loyalty of the many and various individuals
comprising the population of the large trading area surrounding his store. He was anything but an "inside" man,
his interests required that he meet sympathetically all his
potential patrons. In a true sense he was the representative
of the village . . . The merchant's store was the center. . . .

III

*Retailing could be highly profitable. This led to rapid
turnover in small town proprietorships or partnerships as
explained by Professor Atherton.*

Part of this can be traced to the desire of the small
country trader to move ahead in the economic world,
a characteristic of the petty capitalist throughout his history. In the South such men gravitated to planting or
to commercial operations in larger cities. Contemporary
observers were aware of this and frequently mentioned it
in their reminiscences. H. S. Fulkerson, for instance,
settled in the little town of Rodney, Mississippi, in 1836.
This village of six hundred to eight hundred people had
enjoyed an active trade for a number of years and offered
excellent opportunities to experienced storekeepers who
desired to engage in merchandising. Nonetheless, according to Fulkerson, there was a rapid turnover in business:
"Sometimes three or five years business would be so
profitable to a sober and prudent merchant as to enable
him to retire—sell out to his clerks and go to planting,

or to New Orelans to engage in larger operations. I knew
to my own knowledge one house in which, in the course
of twelve or fifteen years, fortunes were made by three
different sets of partners.

— Reading No. 8 —

THE MANAGEMENT
OF MANUFACTURING [8]

*The pressures that led to consolidation and trusts in
the later decades of the nineteenth century are described
by Andrew Carnegie who surely understood the process.*

✓   ✓   ✓

A demand exists for a certain article beyond the capacity of existing works to supply it. Prices are high and
profit is tempting. Every manufacturer of that article immediately proceeds to enlarge his works and increase
their producing power. In addition to this, the usual
profits attract the attention of his principal managers or
those interested to a greater or lesser degree in the
factory. These communicate the knowledge of the prosper-

---

[8] For I, Andrew Carnegie, *Empire of Business* (New York:
    Doubleday, Page & Co., 1902), pp. 153-156. For II,
    "American Arms and Ammunition," *Scribner's Monthly*,
    January, 1880, as quoted in Harold F. Williamson, *Win-
    chester: The Gun that Won the West* (Washington: Com-
    bat Forces Press, 1952), p. 86; and Williamson,
    Winchester, pp. 87, 88. For III, Frederick W. Taylor,
    The Principles of Scientific Management (New York:
    Harpers, 1911), pp. 6-7, 129-130. For IV, Elton Mayo,
    The Human Problems of an Industrial Civilization (New
    York: The Macmillan Company), pp. 178-179, 180-181,
    183.

ity of the works to others. New partnerships are formed, and new works are erected, and before long the demand for the article is fully satisfied, and prices do not advance. In a short time the supply becomes greater than the demand, and there are a few tons of yards more in the market for sale than are required, and prices begin to fall. They continue falling, until the article is sold at cost by the less favorably situated or less ably managed factory; and even until the best managed and best equipped factory is not able to produce the article at the price at which it may be sold. Political economy says that here the trouble will end. Goods will not be produced at less than cost. This was true when Adam Smith wrote, but it is not quite true to-day. When an article was produced by a small manufacturer, employing probably at his own home, two or three journeymen and an apprentice or two, it was an easy matter for him to limit or even stop production. As manufacturing is carried on to-day, in enormous establishments with five or ten millions of dollars of capital invested, and with thousands of workers, it costs the manufacturer much less to run at a loss per ton or per yard than to check his production. Stoppage would be serious indeed.

The condition of cheap manufacture is running full. Twenty sources of expense are *fixed charges,* many of which stoppage would only increase. Therefore, the article is produced for months, and in some cases that I have known for years, not only without profit or without interest on capital, but to the impairment of capital invested. Manufacturers have balanced their books year after year only to find their capital reduced at each successive balance. While continuing to produce may be costly, the manufacturer knows too well that stoppage would be ruin. His brother manufacturers are of course in the same situation. They see the savings of many years, as well perhaps as the capital they have succeeded in borrowing, becoming less and less, with no hope of a change in the situation. It is in soil thus prepared that anything promising relief is gladly welcomed. The manufacturers are in the position of patients that have tried in vain every doctor of the regular school for years, and and now liable to become the victim of any quack that appears. Combinations—syndicates—Trusts—they are willing to try anything. A meeting is called, and in the presence of immediate danger they decide to take united action and form a Trust. Each factory is rated as worth a certain amount. Officers are chosen, and through these the entire product of the articles in question is to be distributed to the public, at remunerative prices. Such is the genesis of "Trusts" in manufactured articles.

II

Nineteenth-century management entered into contracts for unusual types of work such as construction of plant and equipment for which they had no regular staff. Such practice has continued. But many companies also did part of their regular production or sales under contract. This "inside-contracting" died away with the coming of more elaborate and specialized management in the twentieth century. Its value to early industrial management is described in a popular magazine article of 1880.

The contractor is a man of special ability and experience in the particular line of production which he undertakes. Receiving so much per piece, and being held to a strict accountability for quality, he gives his whole thought to the invention and application of new machinery, processes, and tools—in a word, conducting the department with as much economy and skill as if it were his own. Thus, on executing a large order, one device after another for economizing work, reducing the number of "cuts" or imparting a better finish, discovers itself. Though the contractor receives a given sum for his work, he is required to render an account of his expenditures, and the factory gains ultimately the advantage of any reduction in the cost of production. Not a few of the marvelous labor saving processes that distinguish American mechanical production are the result of the contract system in our large workshops. In contrasting this system with that which prevails, even in the country, in manufactories of textile fabrics, it should be borne in mind that the manufacture of guns, and other machinery, consists in the fabrication of a multitude of distinct parts, each of which had its individual character and cost to be considered.

As it had been developed within the Winchester Repeating Arms Company by the late 1870's, the system of inside contracting had the following characteristics. The operations involved in manufacturing gun components and ammunition were delegated to super-foremen who hired and fired their own workers, set wages, managed the job, and turned over the finished parts to the Company for assembly. The Company supplied raw materials, the use of floor space and machinery, light, heat, and power, special tools, and patterns for the job. . . . In addition, the Company paid him day wages at a foreman's rate as a guarantee of a minimum income. If the contractor incurred a loss which could not be traced to his own mismanagement, this was subtracted from his future profits but left his day pay unaffected. . . . Only about half the workers employed in the gun shop during this period were covered by the inside contracting system. In general the Company used its own employees for maintenance, inspection, and assembling.

III

Frederick W. Taylor is widely regarded as the father of "scientific management" from which arose many of the ideas that were applied by companies during the following decades. Taylor summarized his views in a paper read to the American Society of Mechanical Engineers in 1902, but his influence was limited until the publication of The Principles of Scientific Management *in 1911, from which the following is taken.*

✦ ✦ ✦

It is only when we fully realize that our duty, as well as our opportunity, lies in systematically cooperating to train and to make this competent man, instead of in hunting for a man whom some one else has trained, that we shall be on the road to national efficiency.

In the past the prevailing idea has been well expressed in the saying that "Captains of industry are born, not made," and the theory has been that if one could get the right man, methods could be safely left to him. In the future it will be appreciated that our leaders must be trained right as well as born right, and that no great man can (with the old system of personal management) hope to compete with a number of ordinary men who have been properly organized so as efficiently to co-operate.

In the past the man has been first; in the future the system must be first. This in no sense, however, implies that great men are not needed. On the contrary, the first object of any good system must be that of developing first-class men; and under systematic management the best man rises to the top more certainly and more rapidly than ever before.

This paper has been written:

First. To point out, through a series of simple illustrations, the great loss which the whole country is suffering through inefficiency in almost all of our daily acts.

Second. To try to convince the reader that the remedy for this inefficiency lies in systematic management, rather than in searching for some unusual or extraordinary man.

Third. To prove that the best management is a true science, resting upon clearly defined laws, rules, and principles, as a foundation. And further to show that the fundamental principles of scientific management are applicable to all kinds of human activities, from our simplest individual acts to the work of our great corporations, which call for the most elaborate cooperation. And, briefly, through a series of illustrations, to convince the reader that whenever these principles are correctly applied, results must follow which are truly astounding. . . .

Messrs. Gantt, Barth, and the writer have presented papers to the American Society of Mechanical Engineers on the subject of scientific management. In these papers the mechanism which is used has been described at some length. As elements of this mechanism may be cited:

Time study, with the implements and methods for properly making it.

Functional or divided foremanship and its superiority to the old-fashioned single foreman.

The standardization of all tools and implements used in the trades, and also of the acts or movements of workmen for each class of work.

The desirability of a planning room or department.

The "exception principle" in management.

The use of slide-rules and similar time-saving implements.

Instruction cards for the workman.

The task idea in management, accompanied by a large bonus for the successful performance of the task.

The "differential rate."

Mnemonic systems for classifying manufactured products as well as implements used in manufacturing.

A routing system.

Modern cost system, etc., etc.

IV

Taylor saw the managerial problem as one of introducing an engineering type of efficiency. A generation later Elton Mayo gave a new turn to the study of industrial operations by putting the emphasis on morale. After a study of the Hawthorne works of the Western Electric Company in the 1920's, Professor Mayo wrote The Human Problems of an Industrial Civilization. *The following selections are from the concluding chapter called "The Problem of the Administrator."*

Better methods for the discovery of an administrative *elite,* better methods of maintaining working morale. The country that first solves these problems will infallibly outstrip the others in the race for stability, security, and development. There is one important aspect of the employer-employee problems which has persisted through a century of change in industrial organization, in wages and in working conditions. This is the problem which was tentatively stated in the final phases of the interview study at Hawthorne. It may be briefly expressed in a claim that at no time since the industrial revolution has there been, except sporadically here and there, anything of the nature of effective and whole-hearted collaboration between the administrative and the working groups in industry. To "take sides" immediately on an issue such as this and to assign heavy blame to one side or other is useless. The failure is due to our incapacity to define the actual problem with sufficient precision. . . .

In the United States we have travelled rapidly and carelessly from . . . simple social and economic organization to a form of industrial organization which assumes that every participant will be a devotee of systematic economies and rigid logic. This unthinking assumption does not "work" with us, it does not "work" in Russia; it has never "worked" in the whole course of human history. The industrial worker, whether capable of it or no, does not want to develop a blackboard logic which shall guide his method of life and work. What he wants is more nearly described as, first, a method of living in social relationship to other people and, second, as part of this an economic function for and value to the group. The whole of this most important aspect of human nature we have recklessly disregarded in our "triumphant" industrial progress. . . .

The urgent problem of the present is that our administrative *elite* has become addict of a few specialist studies and has unduly discounted the human and social aspects of industrial organization. The immediate need is to restore effective human collaboration; as a prerequisite of this, extention of the type of research I have reported is the major requirement. An administrator in these days should be qualified as a "listener"; many of our *elite* are so qualified, but are not able to relate the various "echoes" they catch in conversation to anything beyond their own experience.

⌐ Reading No. 9 —

BANKING AND FINANCE[9]

I

The Civil War led to a paper currency sponsored by the federal government in place of a vast array of state bank notes. The government paper consisted of gold and silver certificates, issued on the basis of specie deposited in the treasury; legal tender notes issued during the War with no set date of repayment, called greenbacks; and national bank notes secured by government bonds as described below. Business was greatly aided by these uniform currencies which were acceptable at the same rate all over the country. But since the quantity of greenbacks and national bank notes was limited by law from the start, businessmen found the currency too inelastic to keep pace with the rapid expansion of American activity.

The following are the key provisions of the National Bank Act which created a type of banking system, although a very loose one, from 1864 to 1914.

⁄   ⁄   ⁄

[9] For I, National Bank Act, June 3, 1864, Text in *U. S. Statutes at Large*, XIII, pp. 99-118. For II, Federal Reserve Act, December 23, 1913, Text in *U. S. Statutes at Large*, XXXVIII, Part I, pp. 251-275; and Report of Committee Appointed to Investigate the Concentration of Control of Money and Credit, *House Report* 1593, 62 Cong., 3 Sess., 1913, p. 877, as quoted in Redlich, *American Banking*, p. 374.

NATIONAL BANK ACT, JUNE 3, 1864

An Act to provide a National Currency, secured by a Pledge of United States Bonds, and to provide for the Circulation and Redemption thereof.

Be it enacted . . . , That there shall be established in the treasury department a separate bureau, which shall be charged with the execution of this and all other laws that may be passed by congress respecting the issue and regulation of a national currency secured by United States bonds. The chief officer of the said bureau shall be denominated the comptroller of the currency, and shall be under the general direction of the Secretary of the Treasury. He shall be appointed by the President, on the recommendation of the Secretary of the Treasury, by and with the advice and consent of the Senate, and shall hold his office for the term of five years unless sooner removed by the President, upon reasons to be communicated by him to the Senate. . . . The comptroller and deputy-comptroller shall not, either directly or indirectly, be interested in any association issuing national currency under the provisions of this act. . . .

SEC. 5. *And be it further enacted,* That associations for carrying on the business of banking may be formed by any number of persons, not less in any case than five, who shall enter into articles of association, which shall specify in general terms the object for which the association is formed, and may contain any other provisions, not inconsistent with the provisions of this act. . . .

SEC. 7. *And be it further enacted,* That no association shall be organized under this act, with a less capital than one hundred thousand dollars, nor in a city whose population exceeds fifty thousand persons, with a less capital than two hundred thousand dollars: *Provided,* That banks with a capital of not less than fifty thousand dollars may, with the approval of the Secretary of the Treasury, be organized in any place the population of which does not exceed six thousand inhabitants. . . .

SEC. 16. *And be it further enacted,* That every association, after having complied with the provisions of this act, preliminary to the commencement of banking business under its provisions, and before it shall be authorized to commence business, shall transfer and deliver to the treasurer of the United States any United States registered bonds bearing interest to an amount not less than thirty thousand dollars nor less than one third of the capital stock paid in, which bonds shall be deposited with the treasurer of the United States. . . .

SEC. 21. *And be it further enacted,* That upon the transfer and delivery of bonds to the treasurer, as provided in the foregoing section, the association making the same shall be entitled to receive from the comptroller of the currency circulating notes of different denominations, in blank, registered and countersigned as hereinafter provided, equal in amount to ninety per centum of the current market value of the United States bonds so transferred and delivered . . . and at no time shall the total amount of such notes, issued to any such association, exceed the amount at such time actually paid in of its capital stock.

SEC. 22. *And be it further enacted,* That the entire amount of notes for circulation to be issued under this act shall not exceed three hundred millions of dollars. . . .

II

The next fundamental change in United States banking laws was the Federal Reserve Act of 1914. As explained in Chapter VII, the law was designed to give banks access to additional reserves of currency in times of need. National banks had to join the Federal Reserve system, but, as in the earlier law, membership by trust companies and state banks was voluntary, and only a small percentage of them chose to join. The original act has been modified by later legislation, but the essential relationships remain the same.

FEDERAL RESERVE ACT

December 23, 1913

An Act to provide for the establishment of Federal reserve banks, to furnish an elastic currency, to afford means of rediscounting commercial paper, to establish a more effective supervision of banking in the United States, and for other purposes.

SEC. 2. As soon as practicable, the Secretary of the Treasury, the Secretary of Agriculture and the Comptroller of the Currency, acting as "The Reserve Bank Organization Committee," shall designate not less than eight nor more than twelve cities to be known as Federal reserve cities, and shall divide the continental United States, excluding Alaska, into districts, each district to contain only one of such Federal reserve cities. . . .

Said organization committee . . . shall supervise the organization in each of the cities designated of a Federal reserve bank, which shall include in its title the name of the city in which it is situated, as "Federal Reserve Bank of Chicago." . . . . every national banking association within that district shall be required within thirty days after notice from the organization committee, to subscribe to the capital stock of such Federal reserve bank in a sum equal to six per centum of the paid-up capital stock and surplus of each bank. . . .

SEC. 7. After all necessary expenses of a Federal reserve bank have been paid or provided for, the stockholders shall be entitled to receive an annual dividend of six per centum on the paid-in capital stock, which dividend shall be cumulative. After the aforesaid dividend claims have been fully met, all the net earnings shall be paid to the United States as a franchise tax, except that one-half of such net earnings shall be paid into a surplus fund until it shall amount to forty per centum of the paid-in capital stock of such bank.

The net earnings derived by the United States from Federal reserve banks shall, in the discretion of the Secretary, be used to supplement the gold reserve held against outstanding United States notes, or shall be applied to the reduction of the outstanding bonded indebtedness of the United States under regulations to be prescribed by the Secretary of the Treasury. . . .

SEC. 10. A Federal Reserve Board is hereby created which shall consist of seven members, including the Secretary of the Treasury and the Comptroller of the Currency, who shall be members ex officio, and five members appointed by the President of the United States, by and with the advice and consent of the Senate. . . . Of the five members thus appointed by the President at least two shall be persons experienced in banking or finance. One shall be designated by the President to serve for two, one for four, one for six, one for eight, and one for ten years, and thereafter each member so appointed shall serve for a term of ten years unless sooner removed for cause by the President. . . .

SEC. 11. The Federal Reserve Board shall be authorized and empowered: . . .

(b) To permit, or, on the affirmative vote of at least five members of the Federal Reserve Board to require Federal reserve banks to rediscount the discounted paper of other Federal reserve banks at rates of interest to be fixed by the Federal Reserve Board. . . .

SEC. 14. Every Federal reserve bank shall have power: . . .

(b) To buy and sell, at home or abroad, bonds and notes of the United States, and bills, notes, revenue bonds, and warrants with a maturity from date of purchase of not exceeding six months, issued in anticipation of the collection of taxes or in anticipation of the receipt of assured revenues by any State, county, district, political subdivision, or municipality in the continental United States, including irrigation, drainage and reclamation districts. . . .

(c) To purchase from member banks and to sell, with or without its indorsement, bills of exchange arising out of commercial transactions, as hereinbefore defined;

(d) To establish from time to time, subject to review and determination of the Federal Reserve Board, rates of discount to be charged by the Federal reserve bank for each class of paper, which shall be fixed with a view of accommodating commerce and business. . . .

Sec. 16. Federal reserve notes, to be issued at the discretion of the Federal Reserve Board for the purpose of making advances to Federal reserve banks through the Federal reserve agents as hereinafter set forth and for no other purpose, are hereby authorized. The said notes shall be obligations of the United States and shall be receivable by all national and member banks and Federal reserve banks and for all taxes, customs, and other public dues. They shall be redeemed in gold on demand at the Treasury Department of the United States, in the City of Washington . . . , or in gold or lawful money at any Federal reserve bank. . . .

Every Federal reserve bank shall maintain reserves in gold or lawful money of not less than thirty-five per centum against its deposits and reserves in gold of not less than forty per centum against its Federal reserve notes in actual circulation, and not offset by gold or lawful money deposited with the Federal reserve agent. . . .

During the period from 1890 to 1929 when investment bankers exercised their greatest influence in American business, the syndicate agreement for marketing new securities was developed in such a way as to give great freedom to the syndicate managers. The powers granted to the latter imply the difficulty and risk involved in marketing the stock of a new or little known corporation. Fritz Redlich has summarized a syndicate agreement used by the Pujo Committee of the House of Representatives in 1912 as an example of current practice.

✦   ✦   ✦

The parties of the syndicate bought preferred and common stocks of the California Petroleum Corporation at certain prices, each subscriber indicating the amount in cash for which, together with accrued dividend, he wished to be responsible. The subscription implied that the subscriber was liable to make pro rata payments to the syndicate managers for specified purposes. The managers of the syndicate were to have "the sole direction and management and the entire conduct of the transactions and business of the syndicate." The subscribers especially authorized the managers to buy and sell the securities concerned and to manipulate the market at the expense of the syndicate, which implied the repurchase, if necessary, of securities once sold. The managers were bound, however, not to sell below a certain price. They were authorized by the contract to borrow funds by pledging the securities to be sold or themselves to lend thereon (charging interest to the syndicate) and to fix the compensation for brokers, counsels, etc. Moreover the subscribers irrevocably granted the discretionary right to the managers "to consent to any modifications of and to settle the form and terms of the certificate of incorporation of the corporation and the certificates of said stocks [preferred and common] . . . , the voting trust agreement, the name of the corporation and the state of incorporation . . ." . . . The syndicate managers were actually entitled to do each and every thing without being held responsible at all except for want of good faith and wilful negligence. Subscribers were not entitled to receive any securities or the proceeds therefor prior to the termination of the syndicate. If, on the other hand, the managers chose to hand them securities in compensation for payments required, such securities were to be held by the subscribers subject to the control of the managers, to be returned on request for sale on account of the syndicate. Such was obviously a widely adopted practice, regardless of occasional exceptions to the rule. Morgan, for instance, stated before the Pujo Committee that participants in his syndicates did not receive securities. These were marketed by the House of Morgan in their capacity as the syndicate managers. After the termination the subscribers to Morgan syndicates received their share in the unsold securities (as, for example, in the case of the International Mercantile Marine flotation). Morgan made it very explicit that the sale of securities by different parties was to be excluded because "then the market is apt to be bad."

In the old-style underwriting prospectus, the informa-

*tion given the buyer was in the nature of advertising,
designed to sell the security. The Securities Exchange Act
of 1934 governed practices for security underwriting and
trading on exchanges. Market manipulation by false sales
and other devices was prohibited, and a Security Exchange
Commission was appointed to police the markets. The
following excerpt states other stipulations in the law.*

✓   ✓   ✓

REGISTRATION REQUIREMENTS FOR SECURITIES

SEC. 12. (a) It shall be unlawful for any member, broker,
or dealer to effect any transaction in any security (other
than an exempted security) on a national securities exchange unless a registration is effective as to such exchange in accordance with the provisions of this title
and the rules and regulations thereunder.

(b) A security may be registered on a national securities exchange by the issuer filing an application with the
exchange (and filing with the Commission such duplicate
originals thereof as the Commission may require), which
application shall contain—

(1) Such information, in such detail, as to the
issuer and any person directly or indirectly controlling
or controlled by, or under direct or indirect common
control with, the issuer, and any guarantor of the security as to principal or interest or both, as the Commission may by rules and regulations require, as necessary or appropriate in the public interest or for the protection of investors, in respect of the following:

(A) the organization, financial structure and nature of the business;

(B) the terms, position, rights, and privileges of
the different classes of securities outstanding;

(C) the terms on which their securities are to be,
and during the preceding three years have been,
offered to the public or otherwise;

(D) the directors, officers, and underwriters, and
each security holder of record holding more than 10
per centum of any class of any equity security of the
issuer (other than an exempted security), their remuneration and their interests in the securities of,

and their material contracts with, the issuer and any person directly or indirectly controlling or controlled by, or under direct or indirect common control with, the issuer:

(E) remuneration to others than directors and officers exceeding $20,000 per annum;

(F) bonus and profit-sharing arrangements;

(G) management and service contracts;

(H) options existing or to be created in respect of their securities;

(I) balance sheets for not more than the three preceding fiscal years, certified if required by the rules and regulations of the Commission by independent public accountants;

(J) profit and loss statements for not more than the three preceding fiscal years, certified if required by the rules and regulations of the Commission by independent public accountants; and

(K) any further financial statements which the Commission may deem necessary or appropriate for the protection of investors.

⟵ Reading No. 10 ⟶

MANAGERIAL ENTERPRISE[10]

I

The railroads were the first organizations to face the problem involved in the management of big companies by professional executives. Memorandums written by Charles E. Perkins as vice-president and president in the Burlington System show this railroadman's grasp of ideas that were not generally acted upon until the twentieth century.

✓   ✓   ✓

MEMORANDUM OF ORGANIZATION, 1875

The great defect in the management of most of the large Railroad corporations west of Chicago is in the organization. These corporations have grown rapidly from

[10] For I, "Memorandum of Organization, 1875," by Charles E. Perkins in Archives of the Chicago, Burlington & Quincy Railroad, Newberry Library, Chicago, Illinois, as quoted in Cochran, *Railroad Leaders,* pp. 429-430; "Memorandum on Organization" to Thomas J. Potter, May 22, 1872, in Archives of Chicago, Burlington & Quincy Railroad, Newberry Library, Chicago, Illinois, as quoted in Cochran, *Railroad Leaders,* pp. 435, 436. For II, Alfred D. Chandler, Jr., "Management Decentralization: An Historical Analysis," *The Business History Review,* XXX, No. 2 (June, 1956), pp. 173-174, 139. For III, Edmund P. Learned, David N. Ulrich, Donald R. Booz, *Executive Action* (Boston: Division of Research, Graduate School of Business Administration, Harvard University, 1951), pp. 41-42; and Oswald Knauth, *Managerial Enterprise* (New York: W. W. Norton & Co., 1948), pp. 44, 45, 46, 79.

small beginnings and most of them are today trying to operate with the same governing and supervising machinery adapted to very much shorter and simpler lines of Road. . . . Upon the wise management of details the Road must depend for its success in the long run! In years gone by the careful management of details has been of less importance than now, when margins are being so cut down. But what is the actual condition of things? The C. B. & Q. has grown from 400 to cover 1,600 miles (including the Rockford purchase) and we are trying to manage it with one superintendent, one freight agent, one passr. agent and one master of track and one master of rolling stock. Each one of these men has more assistants than he had when the Road was 400 miles long, but there has been no change in the *character* of the duties of each. . . . It is as if a Company of Soldiers should be enlarged into a regiment and the Captain left to do for the Regt. either directly or by clerks what he did for the Company.

MEMORANDUM ON ORGANIZATION TO THOMAS J. POTTER,
MAY 22, 1882

An important question in the management of a large railroad system is, how to get local responsibility on the part of those engaged in operating different arms of the system. It is obvious that, to hold a manager responsible for results, it is necessary to give him pretty full power over the property which he must use to produce these results, both as to income and outgo. It is desirable that the unit of management, so to speak, shall not be too long, and that it shall be homogeneous. . . . On the other hand, it is desirable and economical to have uniformity in many things, and not to cut the system up into too small pieces, locally independent of one another. The unit of management being determined, the officer in command should, in order to keep himself and his men up to their work, be able to know at all times what his road is earning, and what he is spending—and he should have the responsibility for a loss of business as well as for an excess of expenditures. . . .

Very few more men are employed than if they were all under one general manager; but being directly respon-

sible to some one near at hand, they do more work, and
do it better. Not the least among the advantages to be
derived from the division into units of management, is the
fact that the local population in the country and towns
through which the road passes can more readily know and
more often see in person the general manager. This is a
consideration of importance, and is alone a good reason
for not making a unit too large. Personal acquaintance
promotes good understanding and people like to see those
in authority. Again, the President and Vice-Presidents
can, under this system, bring to bear their judgment upon
important local questions affecting any unit more effectively than through the heads of a number of different
departments far removed from the scene of action.

II

*Decentralization, recommended in the previous ex-
cerpts from Charles E. Perkins, became a major concern
of big companies in the twentieth century. Alfred D.
Chandler, Jr., reports on a study of decentralization in
fifty companies.*

↗   ↗   ↗

The fundamental innovations in the major variations
of decentralized administrative structures existing in large
industrial concerns all came in the 1920's. The first and
by far the most significant was that engineered by Irenee
and Pierre duPont in 1921. The two brothers created
simultaneously for the duPont company and for General
Motors the organization that is still the model for companies decentralizing their operations along product lines.
Since more and more companies are turning to product
diversification as an answer to a number of their business
problems, this type of structure will undoubtedly become
even more widely used than it is today. What the duPonts
did for the multi-industry firm, Walter Teagle and his
Standard Oil of New Jersey staff did for the integrated,
single-industry concern. Moreover, besides innovating in
functional decentralization, Teagle pioneered in the
creation of a central unit which could effectively co-ordi-
nate and supervise a number of huge vertically integrated

subsidiaries as well as functional and product-defined autonomous operating units. The final innovation, that of regional decentralization, was initiated by General Robert Wood in 1929. Although it has for obvious reasons not been widely adopted by industrial concerns, the Sears, Roebuck organization has been copied in the decentralization of large financial firms, particularly the insurance companies. . . .

A significant lesson suggested by the experience of Goodrich before 1953 and the electrical firms before 1950 is that a partly centralized, partly decentralized structure creates major administrative problems. The reason seems to be because the role and function of the top managers and the headquarters staff are not the same for a centralized as for a decentralized organization. In the large centralized firm the staff is more concerned with coordinating and inspecting the work of the different departments and less with providing specialized services and advice. In a concern decentralized along product lines the major integrating and inspection functions are performed by the division staffs. This allows the central staff to focus on providing services and advice, particularly in the fields of merchandizing and production, which in the centralized firm are under the virtually complete control of operating departments. . . .

III

The intricacy of pressures within a large corporation, particularly as they affect the top management, are illustrated in the following two selections. The first is from a team of Harvard Business School analysts of executive action; the second, from Oswald Knauth, a one-time top executive.

✦   ✦   ✦

Particularly significant for the top executives was the fact that their own deeds were being viewed by the rest of the organization in the same terms we have already encountered; that is, "What does this mean to *me?*" Men at lower levels of the organization might be basically in agreement with and loyal to the objectives of headquarters management, yet severely critical of the announced policies of management and defensive against them, especially when these policies appeared to be in conflict with local goals. When such a conflict occurred, the man involved did not think, "Oh, I must be wrong." Instead, he thought, "This is one more piece of evidence that management doesn't know what's going on around here." From his own point of view, he was right; for his point of view showed him the conflict, but not the larger goals toward which the management might be working at a different level. Conversely, management might see only the larger goals and not the need for taking the steps and making the operating adjustments that were essential to achieve these goals. Under these circumstances, one could not say that management was "right," or the subordinate "wrong," but only that they had failed to get together.

In addition to scrutinizing management policy from their own point of view, alert subordinates tended also to check policy against management *behavior*. In any showdown, what management did spoke much louder than what management said. . . .

—————

The qualities that lead a person to found a business and bring it to maturity and those that make a good manager are quite different—the former calls for innovation, the latter for statesmanship. Such terms as "rugged individualist" and "economic royalist" describe the owners of the preceding century better than they do the managers of the present. . . .

The degree of success that management must produce to remain in office is surprisingly small. Indeed management must fail obviously and even ignominiously before the dispersed forces of criticism become mobilized for action. Directors are slow to act. This is entirely proper for they cannot upset the entire organizations for every blunder. Their hope is that things will somehow right themselves. Besides, it is difficult to determine whether a bad situation is due to causes beyond the control of management or to lack of foresight. The balance sheet may yield no immediate evidence whether affairs are improving or deteriorating. . . .

For their own protection, [managers] have sought the sympathetic understanding of their stockholders and the public at large. Publicity campaigns have been carried on and annual reports have become veritable fountains of information. The example set by the pioneers in this movement has been followed by many companies which at times seem to vie with one another to see which can tell the most.

This evolution has an unfortunate effect. It puts a damper on imagination and initiative, and makes for an atmosphere not conducive to the taking of risks. Any decision may turn out to have been wrong, and honest mistakes may be twisted into dishonesty by the unscrupulous in litigation. The temptation to yield is strong. This is the more so because managers know that they are dragging their directors into the shadowy area of interpretation of intent. Management is curiously lonely in its equivocal surroundings. Its relations with stockholders are as unclear as with directors and employees. . . .

Thus the function of management is to keep all its operations in equilibrium. Both growth and deterioration destroy equilibrium. Its restoration is a continuous process. Relying upon its experience and its penetrating vision, management arranges and revises policies so that it can survive in the present and face the future with a favorable trade position. Frequently, one policy must be sacrificed for the sake of others. In reconciling conflicting policies, management is more concerned with its future trade position than its present. For today is tomorrow's yesterday.

— Reading No. 11 —

BUSINESS AND GOVERNMENT[11]

I

Business developed in the colonies in the climate of British mercantilism. The state, either British or colonial, regulated business activities with a view to promoting the general welfare. Regulations generally took the form of price and wage fixing, and stipulations as to quality and measures, particularly in the case of staple products such as wheat, corn or hides. The following examples from Massachusetts in the seventeenth century and Georgia in the eighteenth illustrate the spread and continuity of regulatory practices.

[11] For I, Richard B. Morris, *Government and Labor in Early America* (New York: Columbia University Press, 1946), pp. 68-70) Milton S. Heath, *Constructive Liberalism: The Role of the State in Economic Development in Georgia to 1860* (Cambridge: Harvard University Press, 1954) pp. 55-56: and *Statutes of the Realm V,* as quoted in William MacDonald, ed., *Documentary Source Book of American History* (New York: Macmillan Company, 1926), pp. 56-59. For II Heath, *Constructive Liberalism,* pp. 363-364; Oscar and Mary Flug Handlin, *Commonwealth* (New York: New York University Press, 1947), pp. 70-71. For III Louis Hartz, *Economic Policy and Democratic Thought* (Cambridge: Harvard University Press, 1948), pp. 323-326; James N. Primm, *Economic Development of a Western State* (Cambridge: Harvard University Press, 1954), pp. 26-27. For IV, Thomas C. Cochran, *Railroad Leaders 1845-1890* (Cambridge: Harvard University Press, 1953), pp. 191-192, 198. For V, Andrew Carnegie, *Empire of Business* (New York: Doubleday, Page & Co., 1902), pp. 153, 167-168. For VI, U. S. Senate Committee on Education and Labor, 76 Congress 1 Sess., *Hearings on . . . Bills to Amend the National Labor Relations Act,* pp. 2213-2217.

In . . . 1672, the whole question of wage, price, and sumptuary control was brought to a head when the General Court investigated labor and commodity costs of tanners, glovers, shoemakers, and hatters. . . . In regard to the quality and condition of hides and skins used in these three occupations, the General Court acted at once, specifically ordering that searchers be appointed by the selectmen of the towns to inspect hides and skins before they left the butchers' hands. The Committee of Nine which investigated these industries, in summing up its findings, reported that tanners, glovers, shoemakers were all oppressed by the high wages demanded by journeymen, and took occasion further to criticize "the excesse of pride of meane people that will weare no other shoes generally but of the newest fashion and highest price." Hence such people would not work "but for Such wages wt will maynetaine them in this profuse expensive manner." They concluded these mercantilist lamentations with a specific recommendation that a law be enacted providing a maximum sales price for shoes of elevens or twelve at 5s. a pair and other sizes in proportion, "upon penaltie of forfeiting the value of the whole price of those Solde aboue those values." . . . The committee further proposed "that Some effectuall meanes be used to Suppresse the groweing excesse in Aparrell in this Countrey, pride and Idleness beginning to be the prevayling evills and shames of the people especially of the younger and meaner Sorte, and it is feared they are Some of the provoking Sinnes that procure the Frownes of our God upon us."

This recommendation was incorporated by both houses in a compromise plan adopted to meet the labor scarcity during the Indian War of 1675, when the court passed a series of laws for the reformation of "Provoking Evils," with the express purpose of enforcing virtue and avoiding God's wrath. The "Provoking Evils" denounced "the evil pride in Apparel, both for Costliness in the poorer sort, and vain, new strange Fashins both in poor and rich." Its numerous provisions embraced wage fixing, price regulation, and sumptuary legislation. . . . Under this act a new machinery for price regulation was set up; complaints were to be directed to the grand jurors.

The object of the numerous inspection laws was to improve the reputation and demand for Georgia products abroad and thereby stimulate production. Such efforts began with an act of 1760 "to prevent frauds in the making of lumber." It was in the "interest of the colony," ran the law, "that all lumber exported be honestly and faithfully made." Then it proceeded to define and fix the dimensions of all kinds of lumber and lumber products, and to declare certain types to be unmerchantable and subject to confiscation. Six years later, inspection was extended to beef, pork, pitch, tar, and turpentine, and included the specifications of the materials and sizes of containers, standard weights, and grades of qualities and textures. Leather was included in 1768 and tobacco in 1770. Inspection of the latter was introduced to encourage its culture in the province, especially in the back country where it was thought that the lands were highly suitable, and where agriculture was in a backward state owing to the lack of readily merchantable products.

✓   ✓   ✓

The British navigation acts, passed from 1645 on, are too numerous and complicated to explain here. Additional acts of parliament prohibited such things as the erection of rolling and slitting mills in the colonies, intercolonial trade in beaver hats and the chartering of banks. The selection below from the navigation act of 1660 illustrates the language of the acts and some important restrictions.

✓   ✓   ✓

An Act for the Encourageing and increasing of Shipping and Navigation.

I. For the increase of Shiping and incouragement of Navigation of this Nation, wherein under the good providence and protection of God the Wealth Safety and Strength of this Kingdome is soe much concerned Bee it Enacted . . . That from and after . . . [December 1, 1660] . . ., and from thence forward noe Goods or Commodities whatsoever shall be Imported into or Exported out of any Lands Islelands Plantations or Territories to his Majesty belonging or in his possession or which may hereafter belong unto or be in the possession of His Majesty His Heires and Successors in Asia Africa or America in any other Ship or Ships Vessell or Vessells whatsoever but in such Ships or Vessells as doe truly and without fraude belong onely to the people of England or Ireland Dominion of Wales or Towne of Berwicke upon Tweede, or are of the built of, and belonging to any of the said Lands Islands Plantations or Territories as the Proprietors and right owners thereof and whereof the Master and three fourthes of the Marriners at least are English under the penalty of the Forfeiture and Losse of all the Goods and Commodityes which shall be Imported into, or Exported out of, any of the aforesaid places in any other Ship or Vessell, as alsoe of the Ship or Vessell with all its Guns Furniture Tackle Ammunition and Apparel. . . .

IV. And it is further Enacted . . . that noe Goods or Commodityes that are of forraigne growth production or manufacture and which are to be brought into England Ireland Wales, the Islands of Guernsey & Jersey or Towne of Berwicke upon Tweede in English built shiping, or other shiping belonging to some of the aforesaid places, and navigated by English Mariners as abovesaid shall be shiped or brought from any other place or places, Country or Countries but onely from those of their said Growth Production or Manufacture, or from those Ports where the said Goods and Commodityes can onely or are or usually have beene first shiped for transportation and from none other Places of Countryes under the penalty of the forfeiture of all such of the aforesaid Goods as shall be Imported from any other place or Country contrary to the true intent and meaning herof, as alsoe of the ship in which they were imported with all her Guns Furniture Ammunition Tackle and Apparel. . . .

XVIII. And it is further Enacted . . . That from and after . . . [April 1, 1661] . . . noe Sugars Tobaccho Cotton Wool Indicoes Ginger Fustick or other dyeing wood of the Growth Production or Manufacture of any English plantations in America Asia or Africa shall be shiped carrved conveyed or transported from any of the

said English Plantations to any Land Island Territory
Dominion Port or place whatsoever other then to such
other English Plantations as doe belong to His Majesty . . .

*   *   *

II

*The Revolution had relatively little effect on internal
colonial regulation. In the case of Georgia, for example,
an act of 1783 declared all regulatory laws, not re-
pugnant to the state constitution of 1778, to be in
effect. The same pattern is shown in studies of state regulation in Massachusetts and Pennsylvania. Professor
Heath wrote the following of Georgia.*

*   *   *

The largest body of regulation was concerned with
public utilities. This was a broad category and included
taverns, hotels, gristmills, pilotage services, wharves,
warehouses, ferries, bridges, stagecoaches, navigation
companies, toll roads, turnpikes, canals, railroads, plank
roads, banks, mutual insurance companies, insurance
agents, and weighing and measuring operations. Even
some of the services of public inspection were of public
utility nature. Although waterworks, gas, and telegraph
companies belonged to the public utility category and
had a large growth during the 1850's, they were not
brought under public regulation prior to the Civil War.
The characteristics that were most commonly accepted
as defining a public utility probably were the common
necessity of the service, public charter or authorization,
and monopoly. In the case of banks, control of the
money supply constituted the most important feature. It
was not essential that all of these characteristics be present, nor did the existence of any one or two of them
constitute an enterprise a public utility.

The regulation of public utility services dealt primarily
with rates, although it covered usually also some features
of service and even certain aspects of management. It
was largely of the statute or charter type. Rate schedules
for taverns, grist mills, and ferries were established by

legislative enactment during the colonial period, for wharves, warehouses, and pilotage shortly after the Revolution, for bridges initially in 1790, navigation companies in 1801, toll roads in 1808, turnpikes in 1816 and plank roads in 1850. The most extensive and detailed of these schedules were those adopted for wharfage and storage in 1829. Canal and railroad rates were objects of regulation from the beginning, but the schedules were confined to two or three general maximum rates.

1   1   1

III

To speed economic development many of the states between 1815 and 1850 entered into the businesses of banking and transportation. Sometimes, as in the case of the Erie Canal in New York and the Philadelphia and Columbia Railroad in Pennsylvania the state assumed all the costs and operated the property. More often states subscribed to the stocks and bonds creating mixed corporations with varying degrees of state control. The following partial list of stocks sold at auction by the Commonwealth of Pennsylvania in 1843 illustrates the extent of state participation in banking and transportation.

1   1   1

REPORT ON AUCTION OF STATE
MIXED-ENTERPRISE HOLDINGS, 1843

A. Stocks Sold

at Philadelphia, June 13

Company

    Bank of Philadelphia
    Danville and Pottsville Railroad Co.
    Cumberland Valley Railroad Co.
    Schuykill Bridge Co. (Pottstown)
    Schuykill Bridge Co. (Matson's Ford)
    Bank of Pennsylvania
    Union Canal Co.
    Pennsylvania and Ohio Canal Co.
    Chesapeake and Delaware Canal Co.

Springhouse, etc. Turnpike Co.
Schuykill Navigation Co.
Ridge Road Turnpike Co.

At Harrisburg, June 19

Columbia Bank and Bridge Co.
Wrightsville, York, and Gettysburg Railroad Co.
Codorus Navigation Co.
Harrisburg Bridge Co.
Middletown and Harrisburg Turnpike Co.

At Northumberland, June 24

Lewisburg Bridge Co.
Towanda Bridge Co.

At Wilkes-Barre, June 29

Wilkes-Barre Bridge Co.
Easton and Wilkes-Barre Turnpike Company

At Pittsburgh, September 6

Allegheny Bridge Co.
Monongahela Bridge Co.
Big Beaver Bridge Co.
Greensburg and Pittsburgh Turnpike Co.
Washington and Pittsburgh Turnpike Co.

At Philadelphia, October 24

Franklin and Allegheny Bridge Co.
Monongahela Navigation Co.
Chambersburg and Bedford Turnpike Co.
Centre Turnpike Co.

*   *   *

IV

In the mid-nineteenth century private investing interests persuaded the state legislatures to liquidate most of their potentially profitable business holdings. Bank and railroad stocks were sold to private owners, but turnpike and many canal stocks remained in state hands because they lacked market value.

In spite of federal railroad promotion the period from

*1850 to 1870 marks the height of laissez-faire in the
United States. By 1870, however, railroad and factory
problems were generating new regulatory legislation akin
to that of the colonial period. The railroads were the first
industry to come under both state and federal regulation.
The laws dealt principally with rates and were usually
administered by commissions. Railroad attorneys con-
tested the constitutionality of the state laws, and the
United States Supreme Court in the so-called Granger
Cases in 1877 upheld the right of the states to regulate
saying: "When, therefore, one devotes his property to a
use in which the public has an interest . . . he must
submit to be controlled by the public for the common
good. . . ." (Munn et al., v. People of the State of
Illinois, 94 U. S. 113, 24 L. Ed. 77, 1877). A subsequent
United States Supreme Court decision in 1886 interpreted state regulation of rates on interstate routes as
an infringement of the commerce power of the federal
government. By this time, farmer and small business
sentiment was so strong for some control over rates
that in the next session Congress passed the Interstate
Commerce Act. The following excerpts show the reactions of some railroad presidents to state and federal
regulation.*

✔   ✔   ✔

The presidents came to see that if state regulatory laws
could be avoided, then railroad commissions elected or
appointed to administer them were not an unmixed evil.
Ledyard (of the Michigan Central) wrote in 1883:
"Where there are Commissioners to stand between the
railroads and the public much dissatisfaction can be
avoided, and many things made plain." Similarly, if legislation was to be framed, managers preferred that the situation first be investigated by a commission. . . .

Railroad men generally expected more favorable consideration from courts than from legislatures or commissions, more from judges than from juries, and more from
the highest courts than from the inferior ones. In their
attitudes toward the Illinois and Iowa rate laws, the Burlington executives illustrate these beliefs. Walker regarded
the Iowa laws as "hostile legislation" that could not be

dealt with on a reasonable basis. "There is not a complaint," he wrote, "on the whole line of our road by any of our patrons or shippers." In such circumstances the hope lay in appeal to the courts. Walker was sure that the United States courts would sustain the chartered right of the road to control its own rates, particularly if a case could be brought where the decision would not be by a jury.

The decision of the Supreme Court in the Granger cases came as a shock from which Harris, then president of the Burlington, only expected to "rally when the first stunning effects have been exhausted." In 1884 Clarke (of the Illinois Central) wrote to Fish: "It begins to look Pretty Certain that a RR entering the Supreme Court of the U. S. leaves hope behind." But this uncertainty did not alter the belief that the highest federal tribunals were more likely to grant justice to the railroads than were commissioners or state courts. . . .

The Act passed in 1887 threatened the entire railroad rate structure. It prohibited discrimination between persons, commodities, or localities, forbade pooling, and included an ambiguous clause against charging more for a short than for a long haul. Administration of the law was placed in the hands of a five-man commission. . . .

Five presidents from whom there is fairly full correspondence, for the years 1887 and 1888 expressed vigorous disapproval of the Act. Perkins believed that it placed "too much power in the hands of five men, and is subjecting them to too much temptation," and that it was "wrong in principle" to put control of rates in the hands of Federal Commissioners. He also feared rate cutting by roads wholly within one state. Ledyard and other presidents thought that the Act should permit regulated pooling. Fish, perhaps because of his early training in banking, found that "the most objectionable requirement of the Commission related to the financial operations of Railway corporations, that is to say, stocks and bonds owned etc. . . . The connection between such purely financial transactions and 'Commerce among the States' is to me imperceptible."

But, as other writers have observed, until the courts began to demonstrate the weakness of the Act, the presi-

dents generally favored observing its letter. Clarke wrote
to Fish: "The only thing left for the Rail Roads to do is
to largely increase the long haul or through rates. Act
honestly with each other and be patient." "If the law is
not equitable," wrote Ledyard, "the best plan would be
to follow out the advice of General Grant and have it
repealed by obeying it." Perkins's attitude was: "Let us
ask the Commissioners to enforce the law when its violation by others hurts us." Watrous (of the New York,
New Haven and Hartford) said: "We are all interested in
the *bona fide* enforcement of the bill if it can be done,
but none of us are willing to be sacrificed for the purpose
of teaching the lessons of either its success or failure to
the rest."

V

*Prohibition of mergers or agreements producing re-
straint or monopoly in interstate trade by the Sherman
Anti-Trust Act of 1890 was a second milestone in the
advance of federal regulation of business. The law was
probably popular with many small businessmen, and
obviously unpopular with very big business. Andrew
Carnegie's objection takes the fundamental ground that
natural law makes government law unnecessary. Belief
in a "self-regulating" economy was widely held, even by
entrepreneurs who gained from regulation.*

We have had our age of "consolidations" and "watered
stocks." Not long ago everything was a "syndicate"; the
word is already becoming obsolete and the fashion is for
"Trusts," which will in turn no doubt give place to some
new panacea, that is in turn to be displaced by another,
and so on without end. The great laws of the economic
world, like all laws affecting society, being the genuine
outgrowth of human nature, alone remain unchanged
through all these changes. Whenever consolidations or
watered stocks, or syndicates, or Trusts endeavor to cir-
cumvent these, it always has been found that after the
collision there is nothing left of the panaceas, while the

great laws continue to grind out their irresistible conse-
quences as before. . . .

The people of America can smile at the efforts of all
her railway magnates and of all her manufacturers to
defeat the economic laws by Trusts or combinations, or
pools, or "differentials," or anything of like character.
Only let them hold firmly to the doctrine of free competition. Keep the field open. Freedom for all to engage
in railroad building when and where capital desires, subject to conditions open to all. Freedom for all to engage
in any branch of manufacturing under like conditions.

There can be no permanent extortion of profit beyond
the average return from capital, nor any monopoly, either
in transportation or manufacturing. Any attempt to maintain either must end in failure, and failure ultimately
disastrous just in proportion to the temporary success of
the foolish effort. It is simply ridiculous for a party of
men to meet in a room and attempt by passing resolutions
to change the great laws which govern human affairs in
the business world, and this, whether they be railway
presidents, bankers or manufacturers.

The fashion of Trusts has but a short season longer to
run, and then some other equally vain device may be expected to appear when the next period of depression ar-
rives; but there is not the slightest danger that serious
injury can result to the sound principles of business from
any or all of these movements. The only people who have
reason to fear Trusts are those foolish enough to enter
into them. The Consumer and the Transporter, not the
Manufacturer and the Railway owner, are to reap the
harvest.

VI

*Undoubtedly the National Labor Relations Act, in
force from 1935 to 1947, was the most generally unpopular of all government regulations. Some of the most
disliked provisions are stated in this excerpt.*

✓   ✓   ✓

SEC. 3. (a) There is hereby created a board, to be known
as the "National Labor Relations Board," . . . which

shall be composed of three members, who shall be appointed by the President, by and with the advice and consent of the Senate. . . .

SEC. 7. Employees shall have the right to self-organization, to form, join, or assist labor organizations, to bargain collectively through representatives of their own choosing, and to engage in concerted activities, for the purpose of collective bargaining or other mutual aid or protection.

SEC. 8. It shall be an unfair labor practice for an employer—

(1) To interfere with, restrain, or coerce employees in the exercise of the rights guaranteed in section 7.

(2) To dominate or interfere with the formation or administration of any labor organization or contribute financial or other support to it . . .

(3) By discrimination in regard to hire or tenure of employment or any term or condition of employment to encourage or discourage membership in any labor organization . . .

Employers charged that the National Labor Relations Board was hostile to them. "In 95.7 per cent of the cases," said a representative of the National Association of Manufacturers in 1939, "the employer did not win." The following testimony before a United States Committee shows a businessman's feeling against the NLRB.

✓   ✓   ✓

Mr. Pierce. . . . On January 11 we were notified by the N.L.R.B. that Mr. Folio had filed charges against us of having discriminately dismissed eight of his C.I.O. members because of their union activities, and that we had intimidated and coerced all of our employees in their union activities. . . .

Mr. Martin Wagner of the Labor Board stepped into the picture, advising he had a number of affadavits substantiating the discriminatory dismissals and had examined Mr. Folio's membership roll and that he did have a majority of our employees. I might say that we had dismissed or laid off for lack of work about 16 people, and among them we also laid off 8 men who were allegedly members of Mr. Folio's union. . . .

Mr. Wagner declined to submit the reputedly signed membership cards for our check or to submit affidavits after we denied the discrimination charge and requested proof of Mr. Folio's claim to a majority of our employees. This should be corrected: when charges against an employer are brought, the N.L.R.B. investigator should be required to submit evidence of same—likewise the signed membership cards. Mr. Wagner never even checked the reputed names and signatures on the C.I.O. cards against our pay-roll records and signatures.

I might say that when this came up, also I asked for an election and was refused. . . .

Later on other conferences were held by either Mr. Wagner or Mr. Pericelli [an attorney for the NLRB], and both gentlemen proceeded on the premise that everything Mr. Armando Folio said was gospel truth. After the close of one of these conferences, I saw Mr. Folio and Mr. Pericelli in apparent heart-to-heart conversation one hour later in the lobby of the building where our conference had taken place.

— Reading No. 12 —

BUSINESS AND SOCIETY[12]

I

From the weakening of the social force of church invective against avarice and usury in the seventeenth century to the rise of big business in the mid-nineteenth the place of business in society and society's interest in how a man ran his business was seldom discussed. It was, of course, presumed that the rich merchant should help the poor and support worthy causes. Editorial com-

*ment on the death of Stephen Girard in 1831 illustrates
these traditional attitudes.*

The Saturday Evening Post *represented the general
newspaper attitude. Condy Raguet, a Jacksonian editor
of the Banner of the Constitution, editorialized on
Girard's thrift.*

✓ ✓ ✓

. . . this munificent donor considered himself merely
as an agent, or steward, who was to account for the
manner in which he disposed of his vast wealth; and
. . . his anxious wish was to make such a disposition of
it as would produce the greatest possible good . . . he
has discharged his duty, and fulfilled his destiny like a

[12] For I, as quoted in Sigmund Diamond, *The Reputation of
the American Businessman* (Cambridge: Harvard Uni-
versity Press, 1955), pp. 10-11. For II, as quoted in
Wheaton Lane, *Commodore Vanderbilt* (New York:
Alfred A. Knopf, 1942), p. 136 and Henry D. Lloyd,
Wealth Against Commonwealth (New York: Harper &
Brothers, 1894), p. 291. For III, Letters of Charles E.
Perkins to John M. Forbes, February 24, 1881, John M.
Forbes to Charles E. Perkins, March 25, 1881 and to
Edward M. Cheney, April 8, 1881, in Archives of the
Chicago, Burlington & Quincy Railroad, Newberry Li-
brary, Chicago, Illinois, as quoted in Cochran, *Railroad
Leaders*, pp. 434, 339, 340 and Andrew Carnegie, *Gospel
of Wealth* (New York, 1902), p. 15. For IV, Edward
L. Bernays, *Public Relations* (Norman: University of
Oklahoma Press, 1952), pp. 78-79 and "President Edger-
ton's Address," *Proceedings*, N. A.M. (1923) as quoted
in James W. Prothero, *The Dollar Decade* (Baton Rouge:
Louisiana State University Press, 1952), p. 170. For V,
"The Businessman's View," in *How Can a Better Under-
standing of Our Economic System be Fostered?* (Com-
mittee for Economic Development, 1950); and Morris
Sayre, "We Owe It to America" an address before the
Congress of American Industry, December 3, 1948, as
quoted in Howard R. Bowen, *Social Responsibilities of
the Businessman* (New York: Harper & Brothers, 1953),
p. 52. For VI, Gwilym A. Price, as quoted in Eugene
Staley, *Creating an Industrial Civilization* (New York:
Harper & Brothers, 1952) p. 16 and Bowen, *Social
Responsibilities of the Businessman*, pp. 126-127.

philanthropist and benefactor, and left behind him those who for generations will revere his name and cherish his memory . . . Mr. Girard looked upon the wealth and prosperity of individuals as blessings that are given in trust, to be used and disposed for the common good of society.

You would hear people say, "It is a pity that Mr. Girard does not make a better use of his money—he ought to live more affluently, and by that means, give employment to tradesmen and other poor people." It is very certain, that Mr. Girard contributed very little to the support of livery servants, footmen, coachmen, pastry-cooks, French restaurateurs, ice-cream-makers, dancing masters, musicians, play actors, hair-dressers, fancy shop-keepers, jewellers, and many other callings; but his income was not, on that account, less unexpended. His fancy was to set in motion the industry of ship-builders, riggers, and sailmakers, seamen, stevedores, and draymen, and of late years, that of carpenters, bricklayers, brockmakers, masons, plaisterers, painters, glaziers, marble masons, and all the other mechanics employed by him in building houses. What portion of his capital he did not expend, he lent to others to be expended as they might see fit.

II

The rise of the modern corporation with its limitless possibilities for manipulation revived criticism of business methods. When in the 1850's Cornelius Vanderbilt illustrated the possibilities of corporate manipulation, the New York Times *published a description that provided later generations with the ephthet "robber baron."*

If there ever was a man who made his way in the world, it is Mr. Cornelius Vanderbilt. . . . Like those old German barons who, from their eyries along the Rhine, swooped down upon the commerce of the noble river, and wrung tribute from every passenger that floated by, Mr. Cornelius Vanderbilt, with all the steamers of the Accesory Transit Company held in his leash, has insisted that the Pacific Company should pay him toll,

taken of all America that had business with California
and the Southern Sea, and the Pacific Company have
submitted to his demand. . . . [The directors] must
doubtless have writhed under the consciousness of the
true part that they were playing.

*As big industrial business emerged in the eighteen-
eighties and nineties, Henry Demarest Lloyd became the
most popular of an increasing number of critics. The
Standard Oil Company and its virtual monopoly of refining was the target for attack in Lloyd's widely read
book of 1894,* Wealth Against Commonwealth. *This
extract from the book illustrates Lloyd's colorful style
as well as one of the methods that helped established a
monopoly in refining.*

Matthews woke up one morning to discover, as he
had been told he would, that there was no Atlas Company to get his oil from. Corporations may have no
souls, but they can love each other. The Erie Railroad
killed the pipe line of the Atlas Company for the oil
combination. The courts had been kept busy granting
injunctions against it on the motion of the Erie. These
were invariably dissolved by the courts, but an application for a new one would always follow. At one time
the lawyers had fifteen injunctions all ready in their
hands to be sued out, one after the other, as fast as
needed. The pipe line was finally destroyed by force.
Where it crossed under the Erie road in the bed of
a stream grappling-irons were fastened to it, and with
an immense hawser a locomotive guarded by two freight
cars full of men pulled it to pieces. The Atlas line and
refinery became the "property" of their enemy. Matthews'
supply of crude oil was not cut off immediately. He was
tapered off. One of the superintendents of the Atlas testi-
fied in the suit for damages Matthews brought against the
Atlas after it had passed into the hands of the combination, that by the order of the manager of the refinery he
mixed refuse oil with the crude which they sold to the
Buffalo Lubricating Oil Company. Finally the supply was
shut off altogether.

Matthews turned to the railroads connecting Buffalo with the oil country. They all put up their rates. At the increased rates they would not bring him enough to keep him going; they would not give him cars enough, and told him they would not let him put his own cars on the road. Even the lake steamers raised their rates against him. The farmer-refiner was taking his lesson in the course which had driven his first employer to dig oil-wells because "there were restrictions in the shipments." Cut off from a supply by either pipe or rail at Buffalo, Matthews made an alliance with the Keystone Refinery in the oil regions. War was now made upon the Keystone. It was finally ruined.

*   *   *

III

While "Rockefeller and his associates in general maintained a stoical and aloof silence" (R. W. and M. E. Hidy, *Pioneering in Big Business*, p. 209), railroad leaders under similar types of attack prepared defenses. In February of 1881 Charles E. Perkins, Vice-President of the Chicago, Burlington & Quincy Railroad, wrote President John Murray Forbes.

*   *   *

It seems to me the fundamental truth is that Railroad owners no more fix rates charged for transportation than iron makers fix the price for iron or bankers fix the price of money—and if it can be shown that this is true in practice as well as in theory the public would drop the subject and be satisfied . . . Therein lies all the trouble—the belief that rates for transportation can be arbitrarily fixed so that you can regulate your earnings to suit the volume of stock . . . I have been thinking of gathering up facts enough to prove the theory, which I think can be done.

*   *   *

Forbes advised the hiring of a professional writer, Edward M. Cheney, and wrote Perkins in March.

*   *   *

The question of discrimination seems to be the most difficult one of the whole . . . With Cheney you have got to dodge it or make a better answer than has yet been made to justify discrimination . . . I notice your suggestion about having someone whose name would add to any Railroad Treatise we may put out . . . James F. Wilson is already too much weighted down with his Union Pacific connection . . . I do not know how far Carl Schurz name would add to the value of anything we might write . . . If we were sure he would take our side, he has the best faculty of statement or of writing on Political Economy on this side of the water.

✓   ✓   ✓

Subsequently Forbes wrote to Cheney enclosing:

✓   ✓   ✓

A Boston Journal cutting about Nevada which takes the popular and very plausible side as to the wickedness of charging more for a shorter distance than for a longer one which has competition. In this point is the gist of the whole question—it calls for your best study to illustrate it to the ordinary Reader to make it clear that it is right . . . You and I can see this pretty clearly but how show it to the voter?

✓   ✓   ✓

It was in this atmosphere of increasing criticism of big business, and the beginning of Federal regulation of railroads in 1887 that Andrew Carnegie wrote his famous exposition of "The Gospel of Wealth."

✓   ✓   ✓

There remains, then, only one mode of using great fortunes; but in this we have the true antidote for the temporary unequal distribution of wealth, the reconciliation of the rich and the poor—a reign of harmony, another ideal, differing, indeed, from that of the Communist in requiring only the further evolution of existing conditions, not the total overthrow of our civilization. It is founded upon the present most intense Individualism, and the race is prepared to put it in practice by degrees whenever it pleases. Under its sway we shall have an ideal State, in which the surplus wealth of the few will become, in the best sense, the property of the many, because administered for the common good; and this wealth, passing through the hands of the few, can be made a much more potent force for the elevation of our race than if distributed in small sums to the people themselves. Even the poorest can be made to see this, and to agree that great sums gathered by some of their fellow-citizens and spent for public purposes, from which the masses reap the principal benefit, are more valuable to them than if scattered among themselves in trifling amounts through the course of many years. . . .

This, then, is held to be the duty of the man of wealth: To set an example of modest, unostentatious living, shunning display or extravagance; to provide moderately for the legitimate wants of those dependent upon him; and, after doing so, to consider all surplus revenues which come to him simply as trust funds, which he is called upon to administer, and strictly bound as a matter of duty to administer in the manner which, in his judgment, is best calculated to produce the most beneficial results for the community—the man of wealth thus becoming the mere trustee and agent for his poorer brethren, bringing to their service his superior wisdom, experience, and ability to administer, doing for them better than they would or could do for themselves.

*   *   *

IV

It is interesting that while the attacks on big business in general and monopoly in particular during the Progressive Era from 1900 to 1915 produced some individual defenses, such as J. Ogden Armour's book, The Packers the Private Car Lines and the People *(1906) and a special committee on publicity by the railroads, no company public relations departments appeared, and most business leaders do not seem to have seriously reconsidered their relations to society. By the nineteen-twenties the possibilities of basically influencing opinion had been demonstrated by the propaganda of World War I. The interest of a few professional managers in the largest*

*corporations in the new public relations was a step along
the road toward the mid-century social attitudes of business
executives.*

*Edward Bernays, one of the pioneers in public relations
tells how he started his agency.*

✦ ✦ ✦

When I left the CPI [Committee on Public Information]
in 1919, it was logical that, with my pre-war experience
in publicity and press agency and my wartime
CPI experience, I should follow a similar pattern of
activity. With Doris E. Fleischman as my associate, I
began working in the public relations field. We called our
activity "public direction." That was the best name we
could think of at the time. We knew the term "press
agent," of course, but it had bad connotations. "Publicity"
was too indefinite. At least "direction" seemed
to give greater dignity to our work and indicated that
we were interested in the planning and directing phases
of the field—the broad approach to the problem.

From 1919 to 1923 our work broadened out, and we
came to call it "counsel on public relations," coining the
term from the two expressions that best conveyed our
meaning. The phrase "public relations" had already been
used by the public utilities and railroads. We combined
the idea of public relations with the idea of adviser,
substituting the term "counsel" for "adviser" because of
its professional connotations. . . .

One of our first clients in 1919 was the War Department,
which retained us to help with a publicity campaign
designed to deal with the problem of fitting former
servicemen into America's everyday life. This problem
had become a matter of grave national concern in the
spring and summer of that year.

As one result of directed national publicity for the
War Department's re-employment service, the Kansas
City Chamber of Commerce appealed for help to harvest
the wheat crop in Kansas. On behalf of the War Department,
we prepared a statement about this opportunity
for employment. This statement was carried throughout
the country as a news dispatch by the Associated Press,
and within four days after its appearance the Kansas City

Chamber of Commerce wired the War Department that enough labor had been secured to complete the harvest.

✓ ✓ ✓

While big companies came to share some regard for public relations, the classic attitude that business was not responsible for social welfare still flourished in the twenties. An extreme statement of this view is shown in the annual address of the president of the National Association of Manufacturers in 1923, on the subject of minimum wage.

✓ ✓ ✓

Industry should say to society, "Stop your lazy and fantastical efforts to unload your natural obligations upon industry and the law-making bodies. Assume your task to protect the weak and unfortunate by your own self-sacrifices, and through both precept and example teach them the laws of life. Show them that inevitably they must reap what they sow, impress upon them, yourselves, and all others that obligations are more important than rights, and that only through the performance of obligation does any person retain and multiply his rights. Cease your cowardly and selfish efforts to repeal economic and natural law by trying to set up legislative backstops for inefficiency and by legal statutes to shift property honestly acquired by some into the unearning hands of others.

V

Between the 1930's and the 1950's there was a growing awareness by executives that something more than propaganda was necessary for good public relations. The change in attitude by 1950 is briefly described in the first selection from Frank W. Abrams, chairman of the Standard Oil Company (New Jersey) and in the second from Morris Sayre, president of the Corn Products Refining Company.

✓ ✓ ✓

It always seems rather sad to me that we of the industrial and business world deceive ourselves that we can "make friends and influence people" through such things as paid newspaper advertising, pamphlets, and billboards. Some of that may help under certain conditions. But when it becomes the main channel of our effort, I think it is almost an insult to the intelligence of the average reader. We live our relatively sheltered and exclusive lives, away from the home folks, and expect that a paid notice in the paper will hold their loyalty and admiration for us and what we represent. "Free enterprise, it's wonderful," we say, and then we congratulate each other on what a swell "ad" we have written. What I am trying to say is that I don't think that business has a chance to do the kind of job it honestly wants to do, and the kind of a job for which it is trained and equipped—it does not have a chance to make its full contribution to the welfare of all, unless businessmen get out and sell themselves personally to the other major groups that make up the people of good faith in America. Part of that selling is the exercise of conscientious care and restraint in our business, and part is the simple matter of re-meeting the folks. I am sure that too few people really know those responsible in business organizations. We have gone too far down the road of setting up what might be called a business aristocracy, simply by mingling and talking only with ourselves.

———————

Let's be frank about it. If our predecessors in management, two or three generations ago, had devoted a mere modicum of their time to some individual soul-searching about their motives, about their good faith, about the responsibilities they owe to the people—we wouldn't be facing some of the tough problems we face today. . . . An active social conscience . . . and individual recognition of social responsibilities will compel us, as individuals, to test *every* managerial practice, measure *every* policy by a simple yardstick. Not "What does it mean for me," but rather "What will this mean to my *workers as people,* to my *customers,* to my *suppliers,* to my *stockholders,* to the *community* in which my plant is located, to my *government,* to the *industry* of which I am a part, to the *economy* as a whole?" These tests, honestly made, of *every* individual managerial action, policy, and practice, will be evidence of true social consciousness.

VI

*Not only did many leading executives think that the
attitude of businessmen toward society had changed, but
that capitalism itself had become something different in
the United States of the mid-twentieth century. Gwilym
A. Price, president of Westinghouse Electric Corporation,
said:*

⟋   ⟋   ⟋

In examining our industrial civilization, many of us,
I think, make one basic assumptive error. . . . We do
not realize to what extent capitalism has changed in the
past generation, the past decade, even the past few years.
. . .
Ownership and initiative are broadly dispersed in
American capitalism. Management is becoming a profession. Corporations today support a wide variety of
material benefits that they could not afford at a lower
production level. They are persistently, even painfully,
aware of public opinion. They are continually self-
critical. American business enterprise has demonstrated
that it can correct its faults, withstand abuse from both
its friends and its enemies, and continue its dynamic
transformation and growth. . . . The problem is not
easy or simple, but please credit us with trying. . . .

⟋   ⟋   ⟋

*The classic answer to how far corporations were justi-
fied in spending stockholders' money for social welfare is
given in John W. Brooks's statement: "We can properly
help . . . when it is clearly for the pecuniary advantage
of our stockholders that we should do so, as for instance,
if it would raise the price of adjacent lands belonging to
the Co. we could make a donation of land for the location
of an educational institution." In 1896 the United States
Supreme Court suggested a somewhat broader approach
to what might benefit the stockholders.*

⟋   ⟋   ⟋

It is a question, therefore, in each case, of the logical
relation of the act to the corporate purpose expressed in

the charter. If that act is one which is lawful in itself, and not otherwise prohibited, is done for the purpose of serving corporate ends, and is reasonably tributary to the preservation of those ends, in a substantial, and not in a remote and fanciful sense, it may fairly be considered within charter powers. The field of corporate action in respect to the exercise of incidental powers is thus, I think, an expanding one. As individual conditions change, business methods must change with them, and acts become permissible which at an earlier period would not have been considered within corporate power.

Howard R. Bowen, in writing on the social responsibilities of businessmen has interpreted the mid-twentieth century attitude of the courts.

✓ ✓ ✓

The issue is the remoteness or directness of benefit. The courts usually do not question a donation when the employees of the corporation are beneficiaries, nor frequently donations to general welfare agencies and educational institutions. Although American corporations give millions of dollars each year to the American Red Cross and Community Chests, and (during the war) to war relief agencies, no court decisions have been rendered regarding corporate cases on the whole subject of corporate giving—which implies that giving, at least on the scale and for the purposes now practiced, has the approval of stockholders and of the community generally.

As part of the general liberalization of the law regarding corporate giving, legislation permitting donations for certain purposes has been enacted in sixteen states. The first of these laws was enacted in Texas in 1917. These laws vary widely in their content, but all have the effect of extending the powers of corporate managers to make charitable donations. It is evident that corporate practice and public opinion are more liberal than the stated law. It may be safely asserted that the trend is toward increasing powers, and increasing obligations, of corporations to engage in charitable giving.

BIBLIOGRAPHICAL NOTE

Literature about business in America is both meager and limitless: meager in books specifically with this theme; limitless in studies that bear upon it in important ways. For a fairly complete list of books and articles on the business side of the relationship, there are Henrietta Larson's *Guide to Business History* (Cambridge: Harvard University Press, 1948) and Lorna M. Daniells, Compiler, *Studies in Enterprise: A Selected Bibliography of American and Canadian Histories and Biographies of Businessmen* (Boston: Baker Library, Harvard University Graduate School of Business Administration, 1957).

Historical writing on certain aspects of business in America or in biographies of important businessmen is at least as old as Washington Irving's *Astoria* (1846) that tells the story of John Jacob Astor's early venture in a Pacific Coast fur trading post. But the first general survey dealing with the history of business in the United States was N. S. B. Gras's *Business and Capitalism* (Cambridge: Harvard University Press, 1939). Starting in 1931 Professor Gras also promoted and edited the Harvard Studies in Business History composed of a score of biographies of men or companies. Although some scholarly company histories had been written before this, the Harvard series was the inspiration for many similar studies and it has continued under the aegis of Henrietta Larson and Ralph W. Hidy to be the principal collection.

In *The Age of Enterprise* (New York: The Macmillan Company, 1942) Thomas C. Cochran and William Miller attempted to place industrial business in the whole picture of American life. Cochran's more recent *American Business System* (Cambridge: Harvard University Press, 1957) deals with the interrelation of business and society in the twentieth century.

A team of scholars at Harvard, made up of Francis X. Sutton, Seymour E. Harris, Carl Kaysen, and James Tobin, studied the twentieth-century thought of businessmen as revealed in published literature and wrote *The American Business Creed* (Cambridge: Harvard University Press, 1956) in which they evolve a classic business ideology that was probably subscribed to by businessmen during most of American history. They also contrast the ideas of modern professional management with the classic creed.

In 1948 a Center for Research in Entrepreneurial History was established at Harvard under the direction of Arthur H. Cole. The Center was committed from the start to studying the business leader in society as a force in economic development. An initial volume, *Change and the Entrepreneur* (Cambridge: Harvard University Press, 1949) discussed the problems of entrepreneurial history. This was followed by *Men in Business,* edited by William Miller (Cambridge: Harvard University Press, 1952) a collection of essays on the mores and origins of American and some European business leaders. Since then a number of monographs have appeared including Sigmund Diamond's able analysis of the newspaper obituaries of several Americans of great wealth, *The Reputation of American Businessmen* (Cambridge: Harvard University Press, 1955) and Thomas C. Cochran's *Railroad Leaders 1845-1890: The Business Mind in Action* (Cambridge: Harvard University Press, 1953).

The following list is a sampling of various other types of books bearing on the history of American business.

Albion, Robert G., *The Rise of the New York Port* (New York: Charles Scribner's Sons, 1939).

Allen, Frederick Lewis, *Lords of Creation* (New York: Harper & Brothers, 1935).

────── *The Great Pierpont Morgan* (New York: Harper & Brothers, 1949).

Atherton, Lewis E., *The Pioneer Merchant in America* (Columbia: University of Missouri Press, 1939).

────── *The Southern Country Store* (Baton Rouge: Louisiana State University Press, 1949).

Bailyn, Bernard, *New England Merchants in the Seventeenth Century* (Cambridge: Harvard University Press, 1955).

Bridenbaugh, Carl, *The Colonial Craftsmen* (New York: New York University Press, 1950).

Carnegie, Andrew, *Autobiography* (Boston: Houghton Mifflin Co., 1920).

Childs, Marquis, and Douglas Cater, *Ethics in a Business Society* (New York: New American Library of World Literature, 1954).

Cochran, Thomas C., *The Pabst Brewing Company: The History of an American Business* (New York: New York University Press, 1948).

Davis, Joseph S., *Essays in the Earlier History of American*

Corporations (Cambridge: Harvard University Press, 1917, 2 Vols.).

Drucker, Peter F., *The Practice of Management* (New York: Harper & Brothers, 1954).

East, Robert A., *Business Enterprise in the American Revolutionary Era* (New York: Columbia University Press, 1938).

Emmet, Boris, and John. E. Jeuck, *Catalogues and Counters: A History of Sears, Roebuck and Company* (Chicago: Chicago University Press, 1950).

Gibb, George Sweet, and Evelyn H. Knowlton, *The Resurgent Years: History of Standard Oil Company (New Jersey) 1911-1927* (New York: Harper & Brothers, 1956).

Giddens, Paul H., *Standard Oil Company (Indiana)* New York: Appleton-Century-Crofts, 1955).

Hidy, Ralph W., and Muriel E. Hidy, *Pioneering in Big Business: History of Standard Oil Company (New Jersey) 1882-1911* (New York: Harper & Brothers, 1955).

James, Marquis, *Biography of a Business, 1792-1942: The Insurance Company of North America* (Indianapolis: Bobbs-Merrill, 1942).

Jenks, Leland H., *The Migration of British Capital to 1875* (New York: Alfred A. Knopf, 1927).

Jones, Fred M., *Middleman in the Domestic Trade of the United States, 1806-1860* (Urbana: University of Illinois Press, 1937).

Josephson, Hannah, *The Golden Threads: New England's Mill Girls and Magnates* (New York: Duell, Sloan and Pearce, 1949).

Josephson, Matthew, *The Robber Barons* (New York: Harcourt, Brace & Co., 1934).

Knauth, Oswald, *Managerial Enterprise* (New York: W. W. Norton & Co., 1948).

Lane, Wheaton J., *Commodore Vanderbilt* (New York: Alfred A. Knopf, Inc., 1942).

Larson, Henrietta M., *Jay Cooke, Private Banker* (Cambridge: Harvard University Press, 1936).

Nevins, Allan, *John D. Rockefeller* (New York: Charles Scribner's Sons, 1941, 2 Vols.).

——— in collaboration with Frank Ernest Hill, *Ford: The Times, The Man, The Company* (New York: Charles Scribner's Sons, 1954, 1956, 2 Vols.).

Presbry, Frank, *The History and Development of Advertising* (Garden City: Doubleday, Doran, 1929).

Redlich, Fritz, *The Molding of American Banking: Men and*

Ideas (New York: Hafner Publishing Company, 1947, 1951, 2 Parts).

Riegel, Robert E., *The Story of the Western Railroads* (New York: The Macmillan Company, 1926).

Williamson, Harold F., *Winchester: The Gun that Won the West* (Washington: Combat Forces Press, 1952).

A *Business History Review* is published quarterly by the Harvard Graduate School of Business Administration.

INDEX

VAN NOSTRAND ANVIL BOOKS already published

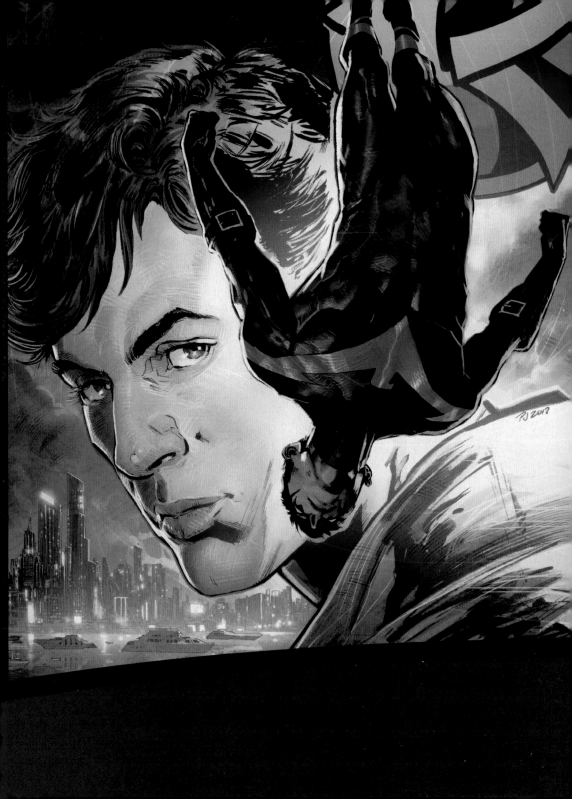

NIGHTWING
VOL.6 THE UNTOUCHABLE

SAM HUMPHRIES
MICHAEL MORECI * JACKSON LANZING * COLLIN KELLY
writers

BERNARD CHANG
JAMAL CAMPBELL * JORGE CORONA * MINKYU JUNG
KLAUS JANSON * PHIL JIMENEZ * MATT SANTORELLI
artists

MARCELO MAIOLO * JAMAL CAMPBELL
FELIPE SOBREIRO * MAT LOPES * ALEX SINCLAIR
colorists

CARLOS M. MANGUAL
letterer

YASMINE PUTRI
collection cover artist

NIGHTWING created by MARV WOLFMAN and GEORGE PÉREZ

CHRIS CONROY   REBECCA TAYLOR   KATIE KUBERT Editors - Original Series
ROB LEVIN Associate Editor - Original Series ∗ DAVE WIELGOSZ Assistant Editor - Original Series
JEB WOODARD Group Editor - Collected Editions ∗ ERIKA ROTHBERG Editor - Collected Edition
STEVE COOK Design Director - Books ∗ MONIQUE NARBONETA Publication Design

BOB HARRAS Senior VP - Editor-in-Chief, DC Comics
PAT McCALLUM Executive Editor, DC Comics

DIANE NELSON President ∗ DAN DiDIO Publisher ∗ JIM LEE Publisher ∗ GEOFF JOHNS President & Chief Creative Officer
AMIT DESAI Executive VP - Business & Marketing Strategy, Direct to Consumer & Global Franchise Management
SAM ADES Senior VP & General Manager, Digital Services ∗ BOBBIE CHASE VP & Executive Editor, Young Reader & Talent Development
MARK CHIARELLO Senior VP - Art, Design & Collected Editions ∗ JOHN CUNNINGHAM Senior VP - Sales & Trade Marketing
ANNE DePIES Senior VP - Business Strategy, Finance & Administration ∗ DON FALLETTI VP - Manufacturing Operations
LAWRENCE GANEM VP - Editorial Administration & Talent Relations ∗ ALISON GILL Senior VP - Manufacturing & Operations
HANK KANALZ Senior VP - Editorial Strategy & Administration ∗ JAY KOGAN VP - Legal Affairs ∗ JACK MAHAN VP - Business Affairs
NICK J. NAPOLITANO VP - Manufacturing Administration ∗ EDDIE SCANNELL VP - Consumer Marketing
COURTNEY SIMMONS Senior VP - Publicity & Communications ∗ JIM (SKI) SOKOLOWSKI VP - Comic Book Specialty Sales & Trade Marketing
NANCY SPEARS VP - Mass, Book, Digital Sales & Trade Marketing ∗ MICHELE R. WELLS VP - Content Strategy

NIGHTWING VOL. 6: THE UNTOUCHABLE

IT FILLS ME WITH A GOOD FEELING.

REMINDS ME OF THE FIRST TIME I EVER SAW BLÜDHAVEN.

THE CITY'S CHANGED, BUT THE TREE HAS STAYED THE SAME.

BACK THEN, I WASN'T NIGHTWING. I WAS ROBIN.

THIS TREE IS A HISTORIC LANDMARK--THE SITE OF THE FIRST COLONIAL COURT. IT'S OVER SEVEN HUNDRED YEARS OLD.

MAKING A CAREER OF NOT DOING ANYTHING I WAS TOLD.

DID YOU KNOW--

YEAH YEAH, FIRST COLONIAL COURT. JACOB DE WITT. WE ALL LEARN ABOUT IT IN GRADE SCHOOL.

YOU BETTER GET OUTTA HERE. THE MAYOR IS AFTER YOUR ASS.

VIGILANTES ARE FOR CRIME. AND BLÜDHAVEN HAS NO CRIME!

WE ARE PERFECTLY SAFE FOR TOURISTS--

I MIGHT HAVE NOTICED.

NIGHTWING IS BAD FOR BUSINESS! HE'S BAD FOR BLÜDHAVEN!

BUSTING UP THAT CASINO WITH BLOCKBUSTER AND RAPTOR WAS NOT MY BEST MOVE...

MAYOR'S AN IDIOT, BY THE WAY. YOU DID GOOD, HERE. NOW GO BEFORE--

I KNOW SHE'S RIGHT. BUT STILL.

IT STINGS.

OKAY, BUT-- WAIT. THIS LEAF DOESN'T LOOK RIGHT--

FINE, FINE, I'LL LOOK INTO IT! SCRAM!

DETECTIVE SVOBODA DIDN'T ALWAYS LIKE ME, BUT YOU KNOW HOW IT GOES.

I SAVED HER LIFE, SHE SAVED MINE.

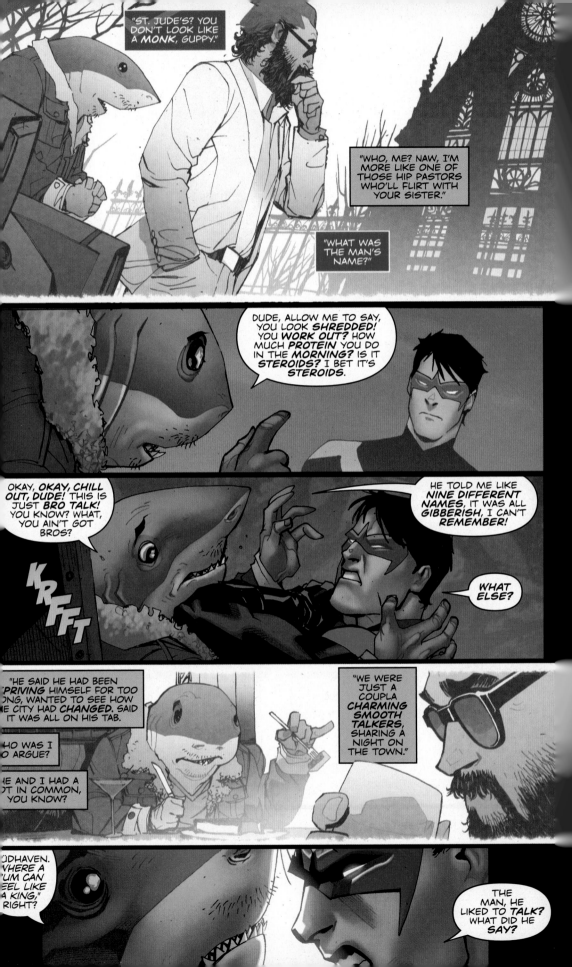

THE UNTOUCHABLE

CHAPTER 1: HUNTER

SAM HUMPHRIES Writer · **BERNARD CHANG** Artist
MARCELO MAIOLO Colors · **CARLOS M. MANGUAL** Letters
CHANG & MAIOLO Cover
BRIAN CUNNINGHAM Group Editor · ROB LEVIN Associate Editor
CHRIS CONROY Editor

BLÜDHAVEN
POLICE DEPT
I'M HIT.
GUNSHOT TO THE SHOULDER.
DETECTIVE SVOBODA PULLED THE TRIGGER.
REMEMBER WHAT THEY TAUGHT YOU.
BREATHE. FOCUS.
BUT SHE'S A GOOD COP.
FIND YOUR TARGET.
MUST BE THE MACHINATIONS OF THE JUDGE.

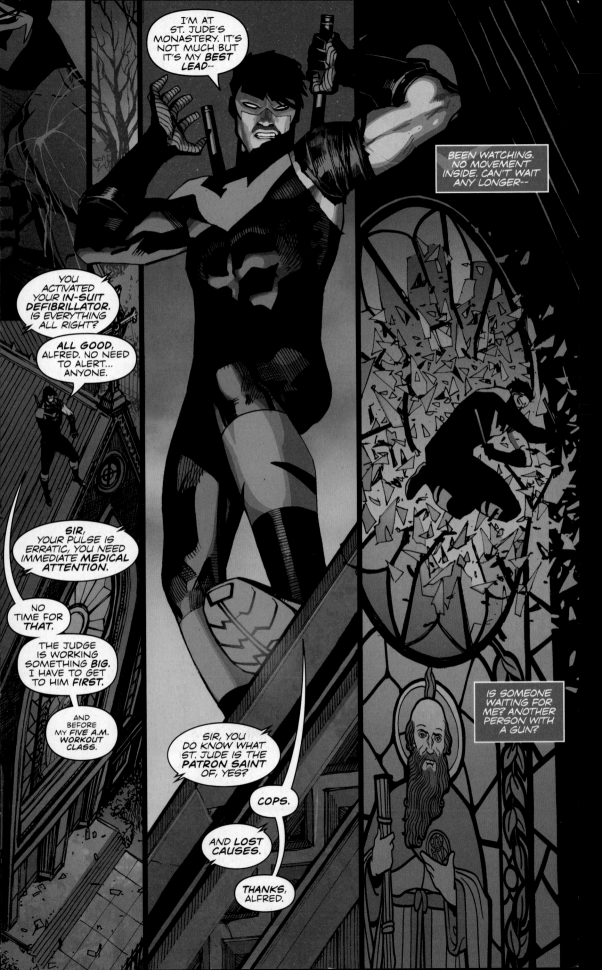

I HAVE TO BE FASTER.

NEW **SCHOOL** OPENING TOMORROW, MAYOR? SOUNDS FUN. SAY, YOU SEND YOUR KIDS TO **PRIVATE SCHOOL**, DON'T YOU?

HOW THE HELL DID YOU GET IN MY OFFICE?!

I'M JUST GOOD AT **MAKING FRIENDS**, MR. MAYOR. WHAT CAN I SAY, I'VE BEEN AT IT A **LONG TIME**!

I CAN BE A FRIEND TO **YOU**, TOO.

"YOUR LIMO DRIVER, **JAY JAY**? GREAT GUY. HE TOLD ME YOUR **SCHEDULE**.

"**SUZETTE**, SECURITY DOWNSTAIRS, SHE SWIPED ME IN THE **FRONT DOOR**.

"YOU EVER TALK TO HER? **SO FUNNY**.

BLÜDHAVEN CITY HALL SECURITY

"YOUR CHIEF OF STAFF, **MALLORY**? SMART. **BIG FUTURE**.

"SHE **CLEARE** THE OFFICE FOR ME."

SNFFFFF

MY FEAR WAS THAT THE JUDGE WOULD KILL, AND DISAPPEAR.

JUST LIKE THE TIME BEFORE, AND THE TIME BEFORE THAT.

THE UNTOUCHABLE
CHAPTER 2: RELENTLESS

BUT NOW I KNOW IT'S WORSE.

SAM HUMPHRIES Writer · **BERNARD CHANG** Artist
MARCELO MAIOLO Colors · **CARLOS M. MANGUAL** Letters
CHANG & MAIOLO Cover
BRIAN CUNNINGHAM Group Editor · **ROB LEVIN** Associate Editor
CHRIS CONROY Editor

HE'S HERE TO KILL.

AND HE'S HERE TO STAY.

"...IN BLÜDHAVEN.

"HOW MANY YEARS AGO NOW?

"THE NIGHT OF THE CITY HALL KILLINGS.

"HE WAS CONFUSED, ASTONISHED.

"COULDN'T BELIEVE HE KILLED SOMEONE.

"ALL OPPORTUNITY, NO MOTIVE. NO EXPLANATION MADE SENSE.

"BUT BY THE TIME THE COPS GOT TO HIM, HE WAS NO USE TO ANYONE...

"THE MURDERER HAD NO CRIMINAL RECORD.

"THERE WAS A GOLD CASINO CHIP ON HIM.

"AND A PARKING TICKET. BLÜDHAVEN PARKING ENFORCEMENT NEVER SLEEPS.

"IT POINTED US TO THE OLD BAILY CHURCH...

CITY OF BLÜDHAVEN PARKING VIOLATION

"...AND TWO GUYS WHO DIDN'T LOOK MUCH LIKE PRIESTS."

"...AND I HAD NO IDEA WHAT I WAS DOING."

TRY *HARDER*, ROBIN. IN THE FIELD...

...FAILURE *IS DEATH*.

"I WAS ALREADY *WELL ACQUAINTED* WITH DEATH.

"AFTER YOU SEE YOUR *PARENTS* DIE IN FRONT OF YOU, YOU DON'T HAVE VERY MANY FEARS LEFT."

THREE MURDERS IN GOTHAM. AND A CRIMINAL IN BLÜDHAVEN CALLED "*THE JUDGE*" IS RESPONSIBLE. BUT *HOW*?

YOU'LL KEEP UP YOUR *TRAINING* WHILE I'M IN *BLÜDHAVEN*.

WHAT?! NO WAY!

YOU'RE *INEXPERIENCED*. IT WAS A MISTAKE TO GIVE YOU THE COSTUME THIS *EARLY*. THE LAST MISSION--

FORGET THE LAST MISSION! I'M READY *NOW*, I SWEAR! *TAKE ME WITH YOU*!

"BUT I DID HAVE *ONE* FEAR.

"THAT I WAS A *SCREWUP*. A LOSER. NOT GOOD ENOUGH.

"I WAS AFRAID *HE* WAS GONNA FIGURE IT OUT. AND THAT WOULD BE THE END OF THAT."

"SO I DECIDED *I* WAS GOING TO BRING IN THE JUDGE."

EASY, ROBIN.

THWAK

"WHATEVER IT TOOK.

"I WAS ALWAYS TRYING TO IMPRESS HIM."

GRAAAAAGH!

"AND MORE OFTEN THAN NOT..."

STOP--!

"...I WAS TRYING TOO HARD."

NICE TRY.

KRAM

AND I'M NOT TALKING ABOUT *THUGS*, EITHER--*REGULAR PEOPLE*. HOUSEWIVES, ACCOUNTANTS...

NO ONE YOU WOULD EXPECT TO PULL OFF A *MURDER*. I DON'T GET IT.

THIS LOOK *FAMILIAR?*

DOESN'T BELONG TO ANY *CASINO*. FOUND ON THREE *"UNLIKELY KILLERS"* SO FAR.

LET ME *GUESS*.

ONE OF THE *CORPSES* WAS LISA NGO. THE *GOTHAM FINANCIER*.

HOW DID *YOU* KNOW?

LOOK AT *THIS*.

THE HARPOON CASINO. "THE *FUTURE* OF BLÜDHAVEN." NGO WAS FUNDING THE DEVELOPMENT.

THE *COUNCILMAN* WHO WAS KILLED AT *CITY HALL?* HE PUSHED FOR A *GAMBLING EXEMPTION* ON THE BOOKS.

THE *DEVELOPER?* MURDERED *LAST WEEK*. THAT'S *HIS BLOOD* ALL OVER THE MODEL. THEY *STOLE* IT FROM HIS *OFFICE*...

THE JUDGE DOES NOT APPROVE OF *GAMBLING?* OR SO IT *SEEMS*...

ROBIN, ANYTHING?

HE'S GOT A NOTE--

Santo Nuevo Voyage #850

Harbor Code 335K-P

I KNOW THE *SANTO NUEVO*. THAT SHIP HAS BEEN CARRYING *RADIOACTIVE WASTE* INTO BLÜDHAVEN FOR *MONTHS*. ILLEGAL *DUMPING*.

AND THAT *HARBOR CODE*-- SHE'S DUE IN *TONIGHT!*

I *ASSUME* YOU'LL WANT TO FOLLOW ME...

"IF IT WEREN'T FOR YOU..."

"...WE NEVER WOULD HAVE CAUGHT UP TO *THE JUDGE.*"

GAMBLING ISN'T THE *FUTURE* OF BLÜDHAVEN! IT'S A *CORRUPT CON JOB* TO ROB THE *PEOPLE.*

TONIGHT? WE MAKE SURE THAT CAN NEVER, *EVER* HAPPEN.

STEP ON IT!

YOU GOT IT, JUDGE!

TIME TO SAVE BLÜDHAVEN FROM THE CASINOS!

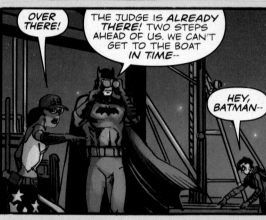

OVER THERE!

THE JUDGE IS *ALREADY THERE!* TWO STEPS AHEAD OF US. WE CAN'T GET TO THE BOAT *IN TIME--*

HEY, BATMAN--

--LOOK AT THAT!

SA

AH, WHAT A *LOVELY BOAT!*

WHAT A *STUNNING* NIGHT FOR VOYAGE!

A REWARD FOR THE MAN WHO KILLS ROBIN!

"I HAD NEVER *SEEN* A KID MOVE SO FAST BEFORE.

"*ROBIN* THE UNTOUCHABLE."

"YEAH, WELL... I HAD EVERYONE FOOLED.

"EVERYTHING THEY CALLED ME BACK THEN...

"'THE YOUNG DAREDEVIL!'

"A LIVING HURRICANE!'

"HARD-FISTED LITTLE SCRAPPER!'

"I WAS PUNCHING AND KICKING AND JOKING ALL THE TIME...

"...EVERYONE FORGOT WHAT I HAD BEEN THROUGH."

OVER HERE!

OBVIOUSLY.

"I WAS STILL A KID WHO SAW MY PARENTS KILLED.

"BECOMING A CRIME-FIGHTER WASN'T A *CURE* FOR MY GRIEF.

"IT WAS AN *OUTLET.*"

WE'RE GETTING CLOSE TO THE HARBOR!

"AND SOMETIMES, ALL THAT PAIN...

"...IT MADE ME RECKLESS.

"AND I WANTED TO BELIEVE THAT ALL THE DARK FEELINGS WOULD GO AWAY...

"...IF I COULD JUST TAKE DOWN THE BAD GUY."

"IF I COULD BRING IN THE JUDGE."

"WHATEVER IT TOOK."

GOTCHA!

"I *HAD* HIM, LUCY."

THOK

WUFF--!

"HE WAS *TRAPPED*!"

GAAH--!

THAK

"BUT THEN..."

THAT'S *IT.*

WE *BOTH* KNEW IT WAS GOING TO HAPPEN *EVENTUALLY.*

IT'S *OVER* NOW, RIGHT?

YOU'RE GOING TO *KICK ME OUT* NOW?

EASY ROBIN

NEXT TIME...YOU DO *BETTE*

"YOU WERE THE SADDEST KID I'D EVER SEEN THAT DAY."

THE UNTOUCHABLE

CHAPTER 3: RUTHLESS

SAM HUMPHRIES Writer · KLAUS JANSON (Flashback),
JAMAL CAMPBELL (Present) Artists · ALEX SINCLAIR (Flashback),
JAMAL CAMPBELL (Present) Colors · CARLOS M. MANGUAL Letters
JORGE JIMENEZ & ALEJANDRO SANCHEZ Cover
BRIAN CUNNINGHAM Group Editor · ROB LEVIN Associate Editor
CHRIS CONROY Editor

CAN'T YOU SEE? YOU'RE PLAYING A *CHUMP'S GAME.* AND THERE ARE NO *WINNERS.*

THE UNTOUCHABLE
CHAPTER 4: INFILTRATION

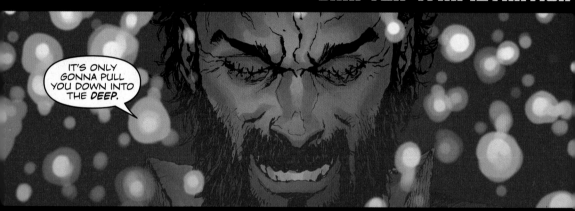

IT'S ONLY GONNA PULL YOU DOWN INTO THE *DEEP.*

SAM HUMPHRIES Writer · **BERNARD CHANG** Artist
MARCELO MAIOLO Colors · **CARLOS M. MANGUAL** Letters
CHANG & MAIOLO Cover
BRIAN CUNNINGHAM Group Editor · **ROB LEVIN** Associate Editor
CHRIS CONROY Editor

UNTIL YOU DROWN IN YOUR OWN *BLOOD.*

BUT I--
÷HURK÷

THOSE WERE COLLEGE STUDENTS--

KIDS!

AND JILL--YOU RUINED HER LIFE, TOO!

÷HUFF÷

÷HUFF÷

HEH... I WASN'T EVEN THERE.

YOU CAN'T PROVE ANY-THING.

YOU MADE HER DO YOUR DIRTY WORK FOR YOU!

VERY WELL--

KRSSSSH

I HAD HIM.

THEN I LOST HIM.

I SEARCHED FOR HOURS.

NO BODIES.

NOTHING.

LIKE HE DISAPPEARED A THE BOTTOM O THE HARBOR.

I'M NOT?! THEN WHY ARE MY BOOTS ALWAYS FILLED WITH SEAWATER?

YOU'RE A MANIAC USING THE LEGEND TO COVER YOUR OWN CRIMES.

AND YOU CAN'T SEE INTO THE HEARTS OF MEN.

YOU'RE JUST A JACK-ASS WHO CAN'T SHUT UP.

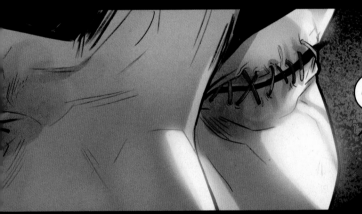

...HOW DO I GET AROUND SO WELL?

IF I'M NOT THE SEA BUTCHER, WHO AM I? AFTER ALL YOUR OBSESSING AND DETECTIVE WORK, CAN'T YOU TELL ME THAT?

I AM JACOB DE WITT.

THE FIRST JUDGE OF BLÜDHAVEN.

THE UNTOUCHABLE

CHAPTER 5: FACE OF

THEN AGAIN... MAYBE NOT.

SAM HUMPHRIES Writer · **PHIL JIMENEZ** (Flashback) Pencils
MATT SANTORELLI (Flashback) Inks · **JAMAL CAMPBELL** (Present) Artist
ALEX SINCLAIR (Flashback) Colors · **JAMAL CAMPBELL** (Present) Colors
CARLOS M. MANGUAL Letters
PHIL JIMENEZ & ROMULO FAJARDO JR. Cover
BRIAN CUNNINGHAM Group Editor · **ROB LEVIN** Associate Editor
CHRIS CONROY Editor

ALMOST DIDN'T MAKE IT THAT TIME.

I HAD THE JUDGE. WE WERE FACE TO FACE. AND THEN HE SLIPPED AWAY.

THERE IS **ONE** PERSON WHO CAN GIVE ME ANSWERS...BUT I HAVE TO USE EXTREME CAUTION.

IT'S POSSIBLE SHE TRIED TO HAVE ME **KILLED**.

GREAT. NO ELECTRICITY.

KLIK KLIK

I'VE BEEN SO FOCUSED ON THE JUDGE, I'VE BEEN FORGETTING MY BILLS.

NEGLECTING THE STUDIO.

LETTING **DICK GRAYSON** SLIP AWAY.

HELLOOOO!

GRAYSON! ARE YOU STANDING ME UP **AGAIN?!** WE SCHEDULED A **TRAINING SESSION**...

ALONG WITH MY CLIENTS.

HMPH. I **KNOW** YOU'RE BACK THERE.

DO NOT ENTER

THIS IS WHAT I *DO.* AND I DON'T GIVE UP, *EVER.*

WHAT'S HIS *PLAN?* I NEED TO KNOW.

PLEASE, NIGHTWING! DON'T DO THIS!

YOU DON'T *UNDERSTAND* WHAT IT'S LIKE WHEN HE *LOOKS* AT YOU...

HE *GRABS* SOMETHING *INSIDE* YOU, SOMETHING *PAINFUL...* AND HE *TWISTS* IT. *HARD.*

AND THEN HE PROMISES YOU *EVERYTHING* YOU *WANT.* BEFORE YOU KNOW IT... YOU'RE LIVING A *NIGHTMARE.* DOING HIS *BIDDING.*

HE CAN FLIP *ANYONE,* NIGHTWING! *NO ONE* CAN RESIST.

NOT EVEN YOU.

LUCY...

≽SIGH≼ HE'S AT THE *SILVER SPRINGS CASINO,* BUT--

YOU'VE GOT *TWELVE BODEGAS* IN THIS CITY. BUT ONLY *ONE* NEAR YOUR *DAD'S ORIGINAL STORE.*

THAT'S HOW I KNEW WHERE TO FIND YOU.

"THE BLOODY BROTHERS OF BLÜDHAVEN!"

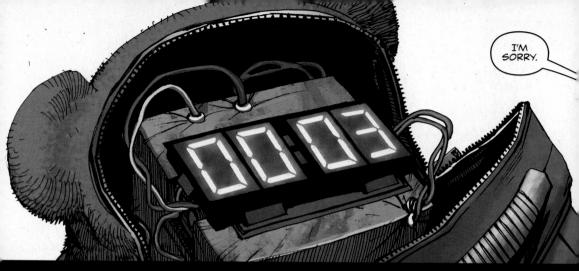

I'M SORRY.

THE UNTOUCHABLE

CHAPTER 6: DEEP DIVE

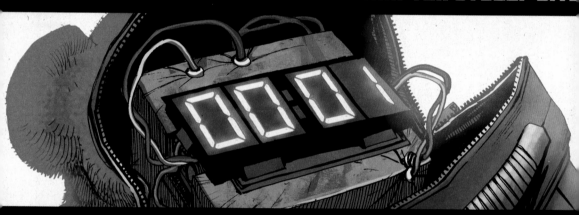

SAM HUMPHRIES Writer · **BERNARD CHANG** Artist
MARCELO MAIOLO Colors · **CARLOS M. MANGUAL** Letters
CHANG & MAIOLO Cover
JAMIE S. RICH Group Editor · **ROB LEVIN** Associate Editor · **CHRIS CONROY** Editor

THE STING OF SALTWATER HITS MY NOSE. MY BLOOD RUNS COLD.

BUT I WON'T COUNT BODIES ANYMORE.

FINALLY. IT'S OVER.

FAILURE IS DEATH. IF I HAD JUST... NOT SCREWED UP BEFORE... ALL THOSE PEOPLE WOULD BE ALIVE.

INCLUDING YOUR FATHER.

INCLUDING MY--?!

BRO, LISTEN. I GOT NO CLUE HOW THE JUDGE DOES IT. IS HE THE FRICKIN' DEVIL?

THING IS, HE COULDN'TA DONE IT WITHOUT ME. THE WORST PART OF ME.

YOU DIDN'T KILL MY POPS. I DID. YOU CAN'T BEAT YOURSELF UP FOR THINGS THAT ARE OUTTA YOUR HANDS.

YOU'RE NOT A KILLER, GUPPY.

WHAT ABOUT THE JUDGE'S OTHER VICTIMS? SOME OF THEM WERE YOUR FRIENDS, RIGHT? CAN YOU FORGIVE THEM FOR WHAT THEY DID?

"LUCY? SHE LED ME INTO THE JUDGE'S TRAP, BUT..."

SO...NOT ONLY WILL THE FEDS REOPEN GAMBLING IN BLÜDHAVEN, BUT THEY'RE GOING TO APPROVE MY NEW CASINO?

WHAT'S THE CATCH?

LUCY. EVERYONE AGREES THERE'S ONLY ONE PERSON WHO CAN RUN THE BLÜDHAVEN GAMBLING COMMISSION.

THE ONLY OWNER IN TOWN TO ESCAPE THIS MESS WITH A CLEAN REPUTATION.

WELL, IN THAT CASE...

SKRITCH SKRITCH

"I'VE KNOWN HER FOREVER."

"IT WAS THE JUDGE WHO TWISTED HER INTO IT."

...I ACCEPT.

"DETECTIVE SVOBODA... WE *TRUST* EACH OTHER. SHE SHOT ME, BUT..."

"SHE WAS FOLLOWING THE JUDGE'S *ORDERS.* SHE COULD HAVE HIT ME IN THE *HEAD,* BUT SHE PULLED HER *AIM.*"

"AND SHE CAME BACK. TO GET REVENGE ON THE JUDGE FOR *MANIPULATING* HER."

YEAH. I MEAN--*OF COURSE.*

THEY HAVE TO TAKE *RESPONSIBILITY* FOR THE THINGS THEY DID, BUT--

NONE OF US ARE OUR *WORST* MOMENTS.

WHAT ABOUT *YOU?*

WHAT *ABOUT* ME?

AHAHAHA!

BRO... I'M SORRY. *BUT!*

YOUR FRIEND *BETRAYED* YOU, AND YOU FORGIVE *HER.*

THAT COP YOU *TRUSTED,* SHE STRAIGHT UP *SHOT* YOU! AND YOU FORGIVE *HER,* TOO.

"BUT YOU CAN'T FORGIVE *YOURSELF?*"

THE UNTOUCHABLE

CHAPTER 7: FINAL JUDGMENT

SAM HUMPHRIES Writer
BERNARD CHANG and **JAMAL CAMPBELL** Artists
MARCELO MAIOLO and **JAMAL CAMPBELL** Colors
CARLOS M. MANGUAL Letters
CHANG & MAIOLO Cover
JAMIE S. RICH Group Editor · ROB LEVIN Associate Editor · CHRIS CONROY Editor

序
"BEGINNING"

LET ME TELL YOU A STORY.

ONCE, THERE WAS A BOY. A WARRIOR OF THE *SOUL*, SEEKING THE CLEANSING HAND OF REDEMPTION.

HIS JOURNEY BROUGHT HIM TO EDO, KNOWN NOW AS *TOKYO*. HE'D HEARD WHISPERS OF A DARK FORCE TEARING THE CITY APART. HE THOUGHT HIMSELF A HERO. HE THOUGHT *HE* WOULD MAKE THINGS *RIGHT*.

BUT THESE FORCES WERE DARKER, STRONGER AND MORE *VICIOUS* THAN THE BOY HAD BEEN AT THE PEAK OF HIS UNWORTHINESS.

THEY TOOK THE BOY. CHAINED HIM IN A TOWER. SWORE TO DRAIN HIM OF EVERY OUNCE OF POWERFUL BLOOD TO FUEL THEIR *CONQUEST*.

THEY THOUGHT THE BOY AN ORPHAN.

THEY DIDN'T KNOW HE HAD A *BROTHER*.

破

"BREAKING"

KABUKI IS REPRESENTED BY THREE *KANJI*. THREE CONCEPTS. THREE *LEVELS* TO THE TOWER.

ON THE FIRST LEVEL, HE HEARD THE BEAT OF WAR.

ROBIN, I SWEAR, IF THIS IS SOME KIND OF *GAME OF DEATH* THING...

THE DRUMS OF THE KABUKI.

歌

THE SONG.

THE THEATER IS NO PLACE FOR WEAK MEN.

ROBIN! IF YOU CAN HEAR ME, I WANT YOU TO KNOW YOU'RE ON BATCAVE CLEANUP DUTY FOR A *WEEK* WHEN THIS IS OVER.

ASSUMING YOUR DAD DOESN'T PUT YOU IN ONE OF THOSE GLASS CASES FIRST!

Ah.

YOU'RE *NOT* ROBIN.

IT IS AN ARENA OF PHYSICAL POWER.

A PLACE FOR AGILE MINDS.

A WORLD DEFINED BY...

...SKILL.

"QUICKENING"

IT WAS SAID THAT THE BOSS KNOWN AS KYU HAD FOUND HIS PURPOSE IN GOTHAM IN THE DAYS BEFORE THE BAT.

YOU MUST BE THE ONE THEY CALL *KYU.*

THEY WHISPERED OF A GREAT AND ANCIENT DRAGON HE HAD CHAINED, DRAINING ITS BLOOD TO FEED POWERS TO HIS GREATEST DAUGHTERS AND SONS.

I LIKE YOUR DRAGON. THAT'S A NEW KIND OF FLASHY.

IN THE NIGHT AFTER HIS CAPTURE, THE CRIMSON KABUKI WHISPERED TO THE BOY THAT SOON IT WAS *HIS* BLOOD THAT WOULD REPLACE THE DRAGON'S.

THE BROTHER HAD HEARD THOSE WHISPERS, TOO.

AND HE HAD COME TO END THEM.

A HERO RUNNING HEADLONG INTO HIS VERY *DEATH* TO SAVE HIS BROTHER.

A FIGHT MY BROTHER COULD NOT WIN.

FOR MY BROTHER WAS RAISED IN THE CIRCUS.

HE KNEW HOW TO PLAY TO HIS AUDIENCE.

A VILLAIN KEEPING ALIVE THE VERY *WORST* OF HUMANITY.

BUT THAT DID NOT STOP HIM FROM TRYING.

HE KNEW HOW TO PUT ON A SHOW.

AND HE KNEW WHEN IT WAS TIME TO TURN A SOLO ACT...

...INTO A *FAMILY* ONE.

WE FOUGHT WITH HONOR AND HUMANITY.

TOOK YOU LONG ENOUGH.

FIGHT NOW. COMPLAIN *LATER*.

SURRENDER, FIEND!

THE VILLAIN HAD NEITHER.

THE *CRIMSON KABUKI* DOES NOT END WHEN THE CURTAIN FALLS. AS LONG AS THE DRAGON BLOOD IN MY VEINS *BURNS*, I WILL NEVER SURRENDER.

WHY WOULD I EVEN *CONSIDER* SURRENDER?

HE THOUGHT HIS SHORTCOMINGS WENT UNNOTICED.

Hmm?

THEY DID NOT.

BECAUSE...

ONCE, THERE WAS A BOY. A WARRIOR OF THE *SOUL*, SEEKING THE CLEANSING HAND OF REDEMPTION.

HIS JOURNEY BROUGHT HIM TO EDO, KNOWN NOW AS *TOKYO*. HE'D HEARD WHISPERS OF A DARK FORCE TEARING THE CITY APART. HE THOUGHT HIMSELF A HERO. HE THOUGHT *HE* WOULD MAKE THINGS *RIGHT*.

BUT THESE *FORCES* WERE DARKER, STRONGER AND MORE *VICIOUS* EVEN THAN THE BOY HAD BEEN AT THE PEAK OF HIS UNWORTHINESS.

THEY TOOK THE BOY. CHAINED HIM IN A TOWER. SWORE TO DRAIN HIM OF EVERY OUNCE OF POWERFUL BLOOD TO FUEL THEIR *CONQUEST*.

THEY THOUGHT THE BOY AN ORPHAN.

THEY DIDN'T KNOW HE HAD A *BROTHER*.

THEY CALLED THEMSELVES THE *CRIMSON KABUKI*.

THEY THOUGHT THEY WERE UNTOUCHABLE.

AND THEY WERE VERY *WRONG*.

JACKSON LANZING & COLLIN KELLY Writers

JORGE CORONA Artist

MAT LOPES Colorist

CARLOS M. MANGUAL Letterer

JORGE JIMENEZ & ALEJANDRO SANCHEZ Cover

ナイトウィング

DAVE WIELGOSZ Asst. Edi

REBECCA TAYLOR and KATIE KUBERT Edit

JAMIE S. RICH Group Edit

Someone like, say, Damian.

He's like my little brother...if my little brother were a tightly wound, highly trained assassin who could kill you with, like, a single sheet of paper.

"OH, HEY, NIGHTWING, THANKS FOR ANSWERING MY CALL AND COMING TO HELP. I REALLY APPRECIATE IT."

"NO PROBLEM, ROBIN. I'M SO GLAD WE HAVE THIS RELATIONSHIP BUILT ON MUTUAL APPRECIATION AND RESPECT."

IT'S LIKE YOU DON'T EVEN KNOW ME.

GUYS! HEY, GUYS!

THE NOBLE, THE OBNOXIOUS & THE INEPT

MICHAEL MORECI Writer
MINKYU JUNG Artist
FELIPE SOBREIRO Colorist
CARLOS M. MANGUAL Letterer
JORGE JIMÉNEZ & ALEJANDRO SÁNCHEZ Cover
DAVE WIELGOSZ Asst. Editor
REBECCA TAYLOR and **KATIE KUBERT** Editors
JAMIE S. RICH Group Editor

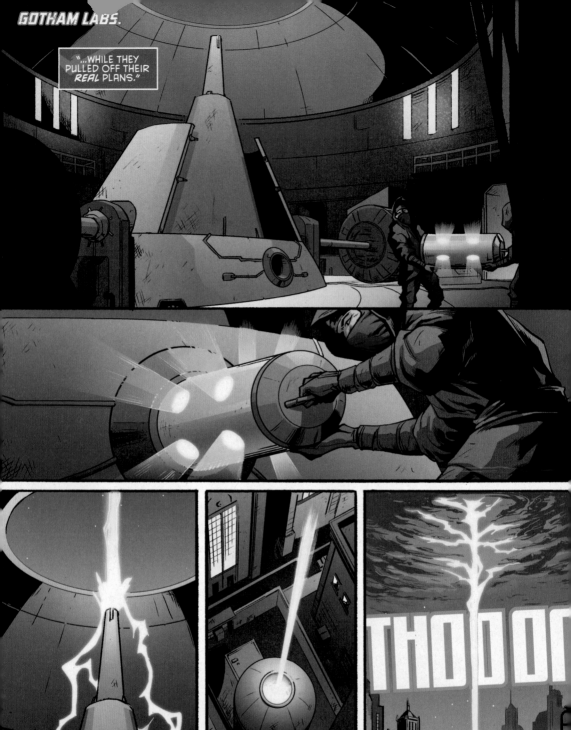

"...WHILE THEY PULLED OFF THEIR *REAL* PLANS."

THOOOM

NIGHTWING

VARIANT COVER GALLERY

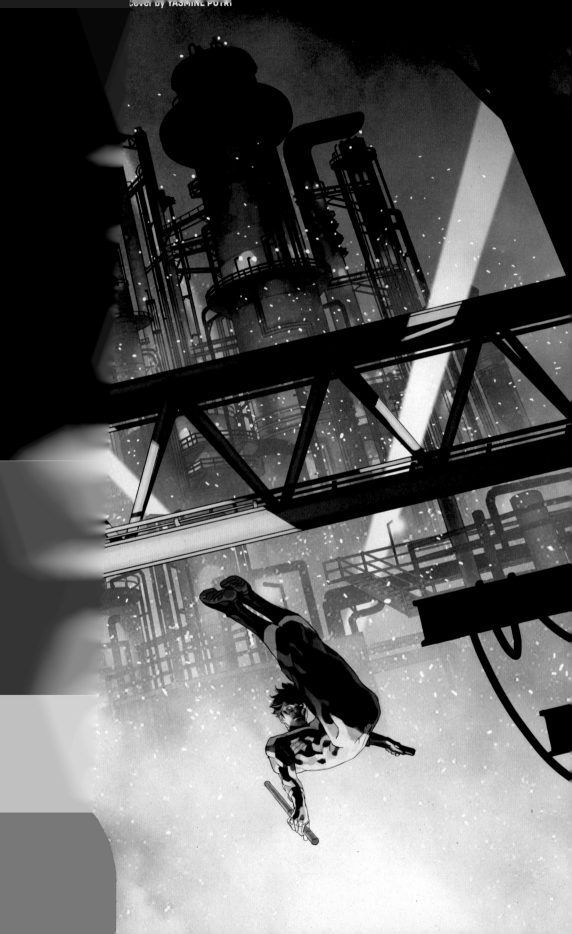

NIGHTWING

THE JUDGE

GUPPY

DET
SVOBODA

WALLACE

HELEN

KING STURGEON

LUCY
(BABY)

LUCY (CEO)

MALLORY

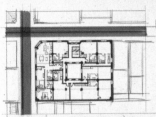

KING STURGEON/GUPPY APARTMENT

-4-STORY WALK-UP
-TOP FLOOR 2 BDRM/1 BA UNIT
-WALLPAPER RIPPED/STAINED
-CEILING STAINS FROM LEAKS

BLUDHAVEN HARBOR

LIGHTHOUSE FORT

THE JUSTICE TREE

NIGHTWING #42 AND #43 COVER SKETCHES
by JORGE JIMÉNEZ

NIGHTWING #42 AND #43 COVER INKS
by ALEJANDRO SANCHEZ